*Frequent Flyer Humor**

And One-Upmanship

Second Edition

***DO NOT READ IMMEDIATELY BEFORE OR
DURING FLIGHT**
if you have the slightest trepidation about flying.

Printed in the United States of America
ISBN-13: 9781492295617
ISBN-10: 1492295612

*Frequent Flyer Humor**

And One-Upmanship

by
James Grosvenor's Nephew
George W. Stewart

*DO NOT READ IMMEDIATELY BEFORE OR
DURING FLIGHT
if you have the slightest trepidation about flying.

Jimmy Grosvenor - An American Man

Preface

Why This Book?

This was created as the antidote for the dreariness of frequent flying. As a former frequent flyer, I've been there, done that, it's happened to me. Frequent Flyer Humor is the remedy.

It is the collection of humorous or incongruous short stories and one-liners, sometimes sophisticated, which ameliorates the annoyances of frequent flying. One-Upmanship because some of the information is unknown to most people. Results range from smiles and chuckles to an occasional knee-slapping guffaw.

It's for the seasoned cognoscenti. The beleaguered, abused, insulted, disrespected and sometimes a little scared passenger who flies too much. A genuine Frequent Flyer has made at least 20 trips per year for at least 3 years. Sometimes much more. You're not a FF just because you sign up for a program. There's about a 100 million of them. "Frequent" is the qualifier. That number is roughly 8-10 million people.

A genuine Frequent Flyer has had one or more abrupt altitude changes that has redistributed the contents of the passenger compartment that were not nailed down. Perhaps his or her beverage, or "meal," laptop.... AND has missed several connecting flights because of weather, mechanical, crew change.... AND has experienced the thrill of an extended final approach that the engineers at Six Flags or Cedar Point would give their first-born to emulate. AND has had his plane hammered into the runway with the force of a couple of Gs.

All of this topped off by waiting for baggage after a long delayed arrival for double the interminable wait because most of the baggage crew had been sent home. This added to the fact that the baggage was to have been carry-on but "the bins are full."

Frequent Flyer Humor takes the reader from reservations to landings with interesting side trips to subjects such as pilot training and flying jargon. It's the largest, most organized collection of this type of information in print. But remember the warning at the bottom of the front cover. **Do Not Read Immediately Before or During Flight if you have the slightest trepidation about flying.**

If you want to have some extra fun, pick a couple of your favorite pieces and entice the flight attendant to read it on the PA whenever you fly. Brightening the unfriendly skies, can't be all bad, can it? Might even catch on.

Table of Contents

ONE

Reservations

RESERVATIONS OF AN AIRLINE AGENT
(After Surviving 130,000 Calls from the Traveling Public)
by Jonathan Lee, *The Washington Post*

I work in a central reservation office of an airline. After more than 130,000 conversations, all ending with "Have a nice day and thanks for calling," I think it's fair to say that I'm a survivor.

I've made it through all the calls from adults who didn't know the difference between a.m. and p.m., from mothers of military recruits who didn't trust their little soldiers to get it right, from the woman who called to get advice on how to handle her teenage daughter, from the man who wanted to ride inside the kennel with his dog so he wouldn't have to pay for a seat, from the woman who wanted to know why she had to change clothes on our flight between Chicago and Washington (she was told she'd have to make a change between the two cities) and from the man who asked if I'd like to discuss the existential humanism that emanates from the soul of Habeeb.

In five years I've received more than a boot camp education regarding the astonishing lack of awareness of our American citizenry. This lack of awareness encompasses every region of the country, economic status, ethnic background, and level of education. My battles have included everything from a man not knowing how to spell the name of the town he was from, to another not recognizing the name Iowa as being a state, to another who thought he had to apply for a foreign passport to fly to West Virginia. They are the enemy, and they are everywhere.

In the history of the world, there has never been as much communication and new things to learn as today. Yet after asking a woman from New York what city she wanted to go to in Arizona she asked, "Oh... Is it a big place?"

I talked to a woman in Denver who had never heard of Cincinnati, a man in Minneapolis who didn't know there was more than one city in the South (wherever the South is), a woman in Nashville who asked, "Instead of paying for my ticket, can I just donate the money to the National Cancer Society?" and a man in Dallas who tried to pay for his ticket by sticking quarters in the pay phone he was calling from.

I knew a full invasion was on the way when, shortly after signing on, a man asked if we flew to exit 135 on the Garden State Parkway. Then a woman asked if we flew to area code 304. And I knew I had been shipped off to the front when I was asked, "When an airplane comes in, does that mean its arriving or departing?"

I remembered the strict training we had received, four weeks of regimented classes on airline codes, computer technology, and telephone behavior. It allowed for no means of retaliation. "Troops," we're told, "Its real hell out there and ya got no defense. You're going to hear things so silly you can't even make 'em up. You'll try to explain things to your friends that you don't even believe yourself and, just when you think you've heard it all, someone will ask if they can get a free round-trip ticket to Europe by reciting *Mary Had a Little Lamb*.

Well, Sarge was right. It wasn't long before I suffered a direct hit from a woman who wanted to fly to Hippopotamus, NY. After assuring her that there was no such city she became irate and said it was a big city with a big airport. I asked if Hippopotamus was near Albany or Syracuse. It wasn't. Then I asked if it was near Buffalo. "Buffalo" she said, "I knew it was a big animal!"

Then I crawled out of my bunker long enough to be confronted by a man who tried to catch our flight in Maconga. I told him I'd never heard of Maconga, and we certainly didn't fly to it. But he insisted we did and to prove it he showed me his ticket: Macon, GA. I've done nothing during my conversational confrontations to indicate that I couldn't understand English.

But after quoting the round-trip fare the passenger just asked for, he'll always ask, "Is that round trip?" After quoting the one-way fare the passenger just asked for, he'll always, always ask: "Is that one-way?" I never understood why they always question if what I just gave them is what they just asked for. Then I realized it was part of the hell Sarge told us about.

But I've survived to direct the lost, correct the wrong, comfort the wary, teach US geography, and give tutoring in the spelling and pronunciation of American cities. I've been told things like: "I can't go stand-by for your flight because I'm in a wheelchair." I've been asked such questions as: "I have a connecting flight to Knoxville. Does that mean the plane sticks to something?" And once a man wanted to go to Illinois. When I asked what city he wanted to go to in Illinois, he said, "Cleveland, Ohio."

After 130,000 little wars of varying degrees, I'm a wise old veteran of the communication conflict and can anticipate with accuracy what the next move by "them" will be. Seventy-five percent won't have anything to write on. Half will not have thought about when they're returning. A third won't know where they're going; ten percent won't care where they're going. A few won't care if they get back. And James will be the first name of half the men who call.

But even if James doesn't care if he gets to the city he never heard of, even if he can't spell, pronounce, or remember what city he's returning to, he'll get there because I've worked hard to make sure that he can. Then with a click in the phone, he'll become a part of my past and I'll be hoping the next caller at least knows what day it is.

Oh, and James... Thanks for calling and have a nice day.

A Senator's aide called in inquiring about a trip package to Hawaii. After going over all the cost info, she asked, "Would it be cheaper to fly to California, then take the train to Hawaii?"

I got a call from a woman who wanted to go to Cape Town. I started to explain the length of the flight and the passport information when she interrupted me with, "I'm not trying to make you look stupid, but Cape Town is in Massachusetts." Without trying to make her look like the stupid one, I calmly explained, "Cape Cod is in Massachusetts; Cape Town is in Africa." Her response - click.

Had a New Hampshire Congresswoman ask for an aisle seat on the airplane so that her hair wouldn't get messed up by being near the window.

Another man called and asked if he could rent a car in Dallas. When I pulled up the reservation, I noticed he had a one hour layover in Dallas. When I asked why he wanted to rent a car, he said, "I heard Dallas was a big airport, so I need a car to drive between the gates to save time."

A nice lady just called. She needed to know how it was possible that her flight from Detroit left at 8:20 AM and got into Chicago at 8:33 AM. I tried to explain that Michigan was an hour ahead of Illinois, but she couldn't understand the concept of time zones. Finally I told her the plane went very fast. She bought that.

A woman called and asked, "Do airlines put your physical description on your bag so they know whose luggage belongs to whom?" I said, "No, why do you ask?" She replied, "Well, when I checked in with the airline, they put a tag on my luggage that said FAT. I'm overweight. Is there any connection?"

After putting her on hold for a minute while I "looked into it," I was actually choking from laughter. After I resumed control of myself, I came back and explained the city code for Fresno is FAT, and that the airline was just putting a destination tag on her luggage.

I just got off the phone with a freshman Congressman who asked, "How do I know which plane to get on?" I asked what exactly he meant, to which he replied, "I was told my flight number is 823, but none of these darn planes have numbers on them."

A lady Senator called and said, "I need to fly to Pepsi-Cola, FL. Do I have to get on one of those little computer planes?" I asked if she meant fly to Pensacola, FL on a commuter plane? She said, "Yeah, whatever!"

A man telephoned an airline office in New York and asked, "How long does it take to fly to Boston?"

The clerk said, "Just a minute."

"Thank you," the man said and hung up.

A man walks up to the counter at the airport. "Can I help you?" asks the agent. "I want a round trip ticket," says the man. "Where to?" asks the agent. "Right back here."

"Flight Reservation Systems decide whether or not you exist. If your information isn't in their database, then you simply don't get to go anywhere."

— Arthur Miller

TWO

Check-In

Why does it take longer to check-in than to fly?

I was at the airport, checking in at the gate, when the airport employee asked, "Has anyone put anything in your baggage without your knowledge?"

I said, "If it was without my knowledge, how would I know?"

He smiled and nodded knowingly. "That's why we ask."

An award should go to the gate agent in Denver for being smart and funny, and making her point when confronted with a passenger who probably deserved to fly as cargo.

During the final days at the old Stapleton airport, a crowded flight was cancelled.

A single agent was rebooking a long line of inconvenienced travelers. Suddenly, an angry passenger pushed his way to the desk. He slapped his ticket down on the counter and said, "I *have* to be on this flight and it has to be *First Class.*"

The agent replied, "I'm sorry, sir. I'll be happy to try to help you, but I've got to help these folks first. I'm sure we'll be able to work something out."

The passenger was unimpressed. He asked loudly, so that the passengers behind him could hear, "Do you have any idea who I am?"

Without hesitating, the gate agent smiled and grabbed her public address microphone. "May I have your attention please?" she began, her voice bellowing throughout the terminal. "We have a passenger here at the gate *who does not know who he is.* If anyone can help him find his identity, please come to the Gate 17."

With the folks behind him in line laughing hysterically, the man glared at the agent, gritted his teeth and swore. "F**k you."

Without flinching, she smiled and said, "I'm sorry, sir, but you'll have to stand in line for that, too."

The man retreated as the people in the terminal applauded loudly.

Case closed.

At the airport my husband and I decided to buy some medical insurance. The clerk at the counter asked us where we were going. "Puerto Plata," I answered.

"Is that in Mexico?" she asked.

"No," I said, "It's in the Dominican Republic."

"Oh," she replied, "you'll have to forgive me. I never was very good at geometry."

Many years ago, long before the resurgence of Midway Airport in Chicago, my boyfriend and I took his mother to the rarely used airport. I believe only one commercial airline flew out of there then, so the place was virtually empty of both passengers and employees. Nevertheless, they had curbside service for baggage check-in, which his mother utilized.

The next stop was at the ticket counter where she was waited on by the same gentleman who had just checked her luggage outside. We then made our way to the gate, where, lo and behold, it was the same guy at the check-in counter preparing to load passengers. How he got there before we did, I'll never know, but he was always one step ahead of us.

I just started laughing and wondered aloud if he was also going to fly the plane. (He didn't). The funniest thing about this, other than the image of him running surreptitiously from each assignment to the next to keep up with us, was that he acted as though he had never seen us before, even though this all took place within fifteen minutes.

I was about to take my first airplane trip and expressed my anxieties about flying to the ticket agent, who reassured me by quoting safety statistics. Feeling a little better, I took his suggestion and chose a window seat. Then the agent handed me my ticket. "Now take this to Gate 22," he said with a solemn face. "That's where we hand out the helmets, scarves, goggles, and parachutes."

It's one of those winter days at the airport in the nation's icebox, a.k.a. Rochester, NY. All flights have been delayed because of weather. We'd all been sitting around the departure gate for our flight to New York City for hours. Most of us have that pinched look around the eyes, but most of us are resigned. That's what happens in Rochester in the winter.

The intercom calls out our flight number for an announcement. Everyone starts to line up at the departure gate counter in anticipation of some sort of news. The intercom says our flight will be delayed yet another hour. The frazzled attendant starts to try to attend to individual questions.

I notice the man in front of me in line is doing a barely perceptible jig. I can see his neck is unusually pink just above the collar of his Brooks Brothers suit. The arm holding his black leather briefcase is twitching ever so slightly. He reaches the counter, and the man uncorks! He goes ballistic!

He demands to know the cause of the delay. He shouts to the startled attendant that he must be in New York for an important meeting, and he's already late. The attendant tries courteously to calm him down. It's an unavoidable weather delay. All flights are delayed, etc., etc.

He just gets redder in the face. He demands to know her name. He shouts for all to hear that he's going to write the president of the airline about this unforgivable snag that's been thrown in his way. Somehow he seems to be under the impression it's all her fault, and it's a conspiracy against him personally.

Miraculously, the attendant keeps her voice down and her courtesy quotient remains steady. The man stomps off, muttering loudly.

I come up to the counter. I know self-control when I see it, and I can admire a textbook case of how to stay cool during a seismic disturbance. I ask the attendant, "How do you manage to put up with this sort of thing?"

"It's okay," she says. "He's going to New York, but his luggage is going to Kuala Lumpur."

A friend of mine had been on the road for several days when he encountered difficulties with his airline reservation. The prospect of not getting home sent him into a tirade, which the counter attendant endured stoically.

After correcting the error, she pinned a bright airline badge on his lapel and told him to show it to the flight attendant just as soon as he got on the airplane.

Anticipating VIP treatment, he immediately sought out a flight attendant and pointed to his badge. She looked puzzled, and asked who had given it to him. "Does it matter?"

"Not really, sir, except normally that tag is used to identify children requiring special attention."

Checking in at Newark one day, the Midway Airlines gate agent was in a surly mood. I watched her verbally abuse almost everyone in front of me in one way or another. As I reached the podium, I took out my pocket Day-Timer and looked at her name badge.

I said, "Good afternoon, Grace, may I ask your last name?" and prepared to write it down.

Somewhat surprised, she looked at me menacingly and asked, "Why do you want my last name?"

I responded, "Because I'm writing a book on the best and worst of air travel. Guess which section you're going to be in?"

— Jack Koestner, jaxson@interaccess.com

I was scheduled to fly from Italy to Spain, where my husband was stationed in the military. As I checked in at the airport, the ticket agent asked me some standard security questions. "Has anyone given you any packages that you didn't pack yourself?" he asked.

I told him that my mother-in-law had given me a parcel to take to her son.

She looked at me very carefully and asked, "Does she like you?"

— snehashis_ghosh

THREE

Baggage

After a lengthy delay at the gate while waiting to depart, the Captain finally came on the PA system and announced, "I'm sorry for the delay, but the machine that smashes your baggage and removes the handles is broken, so the ground crew is having to do it all by hand today."

I used to work in an airport baggage claim area. One afternoon I unloaded some arriving luggage on the carrousel conveyor belt. A few seconds later, the belt jammed when the first suitcase wedged itself at one of the turns. After I yanked the bag free, the conveyor started again, and the only way out was for me to ride the belt up to the carrousel.

I sat with the suitcase on my lap to make sure it wouldn't cause anymore problems. As I slid by on the carrousel, a passerby yelled, "Next time, go first-class!"

I was flying home to spend Christmas with my parents, my suitcase stuffed with gifts. As it bumped down the baggage ramp, it half opened, and my toothbrush fell out. I hastily retrieved my suitcase, but couldn't catch up with the toothbrush. As it continued around the baggage carrousel I overheard a passenger say, "My, that person travels light."

A porter loaded down with suitcases followed the couple to the airline check-in counter.

As they approached the line, the husband glanced at the pile of luggage and said to the wife, "Why didn't you bring the piano, too?"

"Are you trying to be funny?" she replied.

"No, I really wish you had," He sighed forlornly. "I left the tickets on it."

Medicine, cash, jewelry, passports, visas, business papers and other valuables such as cameras should be put in luggage that's checked. This makes it easier for baggage personnel to steal these items and sell them on the black market.

If any of your items are missing from your checked luggage, don't bother filling out the airline paperwork to get your belongings back. Just go to the local flea market and buy your items back. You'll get them cheaper than you paid for them originally, and it'll be quicker than waiting for the airline to buy them back from the same local flea market.

"The scientific theory I like best is that the rings of Saturn are composed entirely of lost airline luggage."

— Mark Russell

Dirty clothes weigh more and take more room than clean clothes.

"The thing I miss about Air Force One is they don't lose my luggage."

— Former President George H. W. Bush

Two elderly vultures decided they would fly south this year for vacation, so they made reservations with an airline.

They arrived at the airport. The clerk looked at their luggage and asked if they wanted to check in as baggage the two dead raccoons they brought with them to snack on.

"No," the vultures said. "They're carrion."

If your carry-on baggage won't fit in the overhead compartments, please ram, cram or jam it under the seat in front of you.

The less carry-on luggage space available on an aircraft, the more carry-on luggage passengers will bring aboard.

"Ladies and gentlemen, I'd like to apologize for the delay. It's crucial to the company that we provide the same service to all of our customers. The ground crew was on break. We had to wait for them to return to insure that the right number of bags were sent to the wrong location."

The following was reported to be an actual boarding announcement made by a gate agent in MIA in December.

"Ladies and gentlemen, thank you for your patience. We're ready to begin boarding Flight 1234 with service from Miami to Atlanta. Due to a weight problem with the aircraft, we are going to limit you to one piece of carry-on luggage. Any additional items will have to be checked."

FOUR

Boarding

Screener: "Next!"

Osama: "Hello, infidel! I am going to kill you with a bomb I have in my luggage. It is wired so that you will die painfully with images of imploding kittens chasing you all the way to hell. Failing that, I will shoot you with this gun."

Screener: "Ha ha. You people are a riot, you know? Seriously, I'll be looking for you on Leno. If you don't make it big, there's just no sense on this marble in space, I say."

Osama: "Who is this Leno? Is he also infidel? I'll kill him, too. Where is he?"

Screener: "Geeze, give it a rest. Next!"

— Christobol

A woman went to the airport for a flight to Omaha. She joined the long line at the security checkpoint for Concourse B and waited. By the time she reached the head of the line, it was clear that she would miss her flight if it took off as scheduled.

The guard took a look at her ticket, and said, "I'm sorry. You've got a problem here."

"Yes." she sighed. "It looks like I won't make this flight to Omaha."

"No," the guard explained. "This is the line for missing the flight to Houston. The line for missing your flight to Omaha is at Concourse C."

— Kent B. Van Cleave

Traveling during a holiday period can be especially exasperating. Our flight had been delayed repeatedly, and passengers in the boarding area were tired and cranky. The airline staff tried to maintain good humor, but when the plane was finally ready, one attendant's feelings were obvious. "We're now prepared to board Flight 128," he announced. "We'll pre-board children traveling alone, parents with small children and the families of husbands who are acting like children."

The thorough search of all her belongings, and her person, finally brought a woman to a boil. "This is absolutely astonishing! You might as well be raping me!"

"I don't think so, Ma'am," replied the FAA security guard. "The most we're allowed to do is a nice slow cavity search."

— Kent B. Van Cleave

The long wait at airport security was tough on the five-year-old boy. To keep him from making a disturbance, his mother decided to distract him with a civics lesson.

"Johnny, do you know what's special about America?"

"No." He pouted.

"In America, everyone is free to do things, go places, own whatever they want.... Anything except hurt other people."

Johnny looked ahead at the people being searched by the airport security guards and nodded. "I think I want to go to America."

— Kent B. Van Cleave

My sister adopted a scraggly black puppy just before she was to catch a flight from Kansas to Florida. She made special arrangements with the airline to take her new pet on the plane.

At the airport, my sister prepared to board carrying the puppy in a case tucked under her arm. To the amusement of fellow travelers, she was wearing a T-shirt that read:

"Dear Auntie Em,
Hate the farm
Hate Kansas
Taking the dog
Dorothy."

We were changing planes at Atlanta's Hartsfield Airport and found ourselves coping with long distances between gates. Gratefully, we headed toward a moving sidewalk.

As we were about to step onto it, a grizzled gent in a cowboy hat and boots approached. Wearily shifting the two bulky bags he was toting, he asked, "Can you tell me if this here sidewalk goes to Houston?"

While on duty as a ground hostess at Jan Smuts Airport, Johannesburg, South Africa, I was directing passengers to the bus that would take them from the terminal building to the aircraft. I noticed a rather upset elderly woman, apparently on her first air trip. When her turn came to board the bus, she tried to leave the queue. "You're going to Durban, ma'am?" I asked her.

"Yes," she replied, "but for what that ticket cost me, certainly not by bus."

A few days after Christmas, a mother was working in the kitchen listening to her son playing with his new airplane in the living room. She heard her son say, "All of you sons of bitches get the hell off the plane now, 'cause this is the last stop! And all of you sons of bitches who are getting on, get your asses in the plane, 'cause we're going to take-off now."

The mother went in and told her son, "We don't use that kind of language in this house. Now I want you to go to your room. You're to stay there for *two hours!* When you come out, you may play with your plane, but I want you to use nice language."

Two hours later, the son comes out of the bedroom and resumes playing with his plane. Soon the mother heard her son say, "All passengers who are deplaning, please remember to take all of your belongings with you. We thank you for flying with us today and hope your trip was a pleasant one. We hope you'll fly with us again soon."

She hears the little boy continue, "For those of you just boarding, we ask you to stow all of your hand luggage under your seat. Remember, there's no smoking on the plane. We hope you'll have a pleasant and relaxing journey with us today."

As the mother began to smile, the child added, "For those of you who are pissed off about the *two hour* delay, please see the bitch in the kitchen."

My husband and I had a stop-over in Toronto before continuing to our destination on a commuter flight. It was a rainy night, and we weren't looking forward to the bus ride and walk required to board the small de Havilland airplane. After a long wait the flight attendant finally announced, "Ladies and gentlemen, we're sorry for the delay. Air Canada Commuter Flight 1143 is now unloading. We are waiting for our passengers to be run over by the bus."

Passengers waiting for a flight began to get anxious when the airplane hadn't arrived half an hour after it was scheduled to depart. The harried agent finally told us that our plane had been diverted and that arrangements had been made for us to travel with a rival airline.

By the time we sprinted to the other side of the terminal, frustration levels were high. Finally we were airborne, and drinks were served. A passenger complained that the other airline served complimentary peanuts. A flight attendant lightened the mood considerably when she quipped, "With them you get peanuts. With us you get transportation!"

When I played with a symphony orchestra, our union reached an agreement with a major airline about which instruments we could carry on board and which had to be shipped as luggage. A cellist was dismayed to find that his delicate, expensive wood instrument was to be consigned to the rough handling and cold temperatures of the baggage hold. He neatly solved the problem.

Cello in hand, he approached the flight attendant at the gate and asked, "May I bring my clarinet on board?" Scanning her list, she replied, "Clarinets are okay, have a good trip," and, smiling, waved him on.

A nun is walking through an airport to catch a plane to the Vatican. As she rounds the corner to her gate, she sees a machine with a sign that reads, *Your Weight and Fortune - 5 Cents.*

The nun doesn't believe in such things; however, she goes over to the machine and inserts a nickel. A card comes out which says, "You are a nun, you weigh 125 lbs. and before you board your plane, you will pass gas." The nun is unimpressed and proceeds on to her gate. Ten seconds later she rips a window-rattling blast of gas. She's naturally shocked and goes back to the machine.

With another nickel she gets a card that says, "You are a nun, you weigh 125 lbs. and before you board your plane, you will be raped." The nun laughs (because who in the world would rape a nun) and heads for her plane. Ten seconds later a masked man jumps out from behind a corner, throws her on the floor, throws one to her, and runs away.

The nun is flabbergasted and runs back to the machine to see what else her life has in store for her. The next card comes out with the message, "You are a nun, you weigh 125 lbs. and with all of your farting and f**king around, you missed your plane!"

An exhibitionist was preparing to board a flight to Chicago. As he approached the open door of the plane at the end of the jet way, a very attractive flight attendant was collecting boarding passes. As she reached toward him for his boarding pass, he opened his raincoat and exposed himself.

"I'm sorry, sir," she said politely, "but you have to show your ticket, not your stub."

There were three priests in an airport, all wanting to go home to Pittsburgh. Behind the ticket counter, was a well-endowed, absolutely stunning ticket agent. The priests were all in embarrassing new territory, so they drew straws to determine who would get the tickets.

The first priest approached the window. "Young lady," he began, "I would like three pickets to Titsburg." whereupon he completely lost his composure and fled.

The second priest approached. "Young lady, I would like three tickets to Pittsburgh," he began, "and I would like the change in nipples and dimes." So, of course, he also fled.

Then came the third. "Young lady, I would like three tickets to Pittsburgh, and I would like the change in nickels and dimes. And I must say," He continued, "If you insist on dressing like that, when you get to the Pearly Gates; St. Finger's going to shake his peter at you."

I recently took a domestic flight in Egypt on their national carrier, Egypt Air. As I boarded the aging 737, I looked over the door at the frame where the airworthiness and registration certificates are normally found. Instead, the carrier had placed a copy of the Koran there. Made me feel much safer!

I was in the VIP lounge last week en route to Seattle. While in the lounge, I noticed Bill Gates sitting on the chesterfield enjoying a cognac. I was meeting with a very important client who was also flying to Seattle with me, but she was running a bit late.

I approached Mr. Gates and introduced myself. I explained to him that I was conducting some important business and how much I would appreciate it if he could throw a quick "Hello, Chris" at me when I was with my client. He agreed.

Ten minutes later while I was conversing with my client, I felt a tap on my shoulder. It was Bill Gates. I turned around and looked up at him. He said, "Hi, Chris, what's happening?"

To which I replied, "F**k off, Gates. I'm in a meeting."

A peppery woman at the airline ticket counter was complaining about the delay in the departure of her flight. "Young man," she snapped at the reservations clerk, "The way you people run this airline, a witch on a janitor's broom could get there faster."

"Madam," the clerk said, with just a hint of a smile, "the runways are clear."

While taxiing past aircraft stands and noticing some passengers boarding the rear entrance of a Finnair DC 9, the Captain remarked to the first officer, "Look at all those people disappearing into Finnair."

FIVE

Passengers

"If God wanted us to fly, He would have given us tickets."
— Mel Brooks

"Hello, and welcome to Alaska Flight 438 to San Francisco. If you're going to San Francisco, you're in the right place. If you're not going to San Francisco, you're about to have a really long evening.

We'd like to tell you now about some important safety features of this aircraft. The most important safety feature we have aboard this plane is the flight attendant. Please look at one now.

There are five exits aboard this plane: two at the front, two over the wings, and one out the plane's rear end. If you're seated in one of the exit rows, please don't store your bags by your feet. That would be a really bad idea.

Please take a moment, look around, and find the nearest exit. Count the rows of seats between you and the exit. In the event the need arises to find one, trust me, you'll be glad you did. We also have pretty blinking lights on the floor that will blink in the direction of the exits. White ones along the normal rows and pretty red ones at the exit rows.

In the event of a loss of cabin pressure, these baggy things will drop down over your head. You stick it over your nose and mouth like the flight attendant is doing now. The bag won't inflate, but there's oxygen there, I promise. If you're sitting next to a small child, or someone who's acting like a small child, please do us all a favor and put on your mask first. If you're traveling with two or more children, please take a moment now to decide which is your favorite. Help that one first, then work your way down.

In the seat pocket in front of you is a pamphlet about the safety features of this plane. I usually use it as a fan when I'm having my own personal summer. It also has pretty pictures. Please take it out and play with it now.

Please take a moment now to make sure your seat belts are fastened low and tight about your waist. To fasten the belt, insert the metal tab into the buckle. To release, it's a pulley thing. Not a pushy thing like your car because you're in an airplane. *Hello!*

There's no smoking in the cabin on this flight. There's also no smoking in the lavatories. If we see smoke coming from the lavatories, we'll assume you're on fire and put you out. This is a free service we provide.

There are two smoking sections on this flight, one outside each wing exit. We do have a movie in the smoking sections tonight. Hold on; let me check what it is. Oh, here it is; the movie tonight is… *Gone with the Wind.*

In a moment, we will be turning off the cabin lights, and it's going to get really dark, really fast. If you're afraid of the dark, now would be a good time to reach up and press the yellow button. The yellow button turns on your reading light. Please don't press the orange button unless you absolutely have to. The orange button is your seat ejection button.

We're glad to have you with us on board this flight. Thank you for choosing Alaska Air, and giving us your business and your money. If there's anything we can do to make you more comfortable, please don't hesitate to ask.

And if you all weren't strapped in, you would have given me a standing ovation, wouldn't you?"

On a flight to New York the flight attendant said to a lady sitting in first class, "Ma'am, I'm afraid you'll have to sit in the back since you have a coach ticket."

The young lady responded, "Listen, I'm a beautiful blonde, I'm going to N.Y. and I'm sitting in first class."

The two argued for a while, but finally the flight attendant got the first officer who came and said, "Ma'am, I'm afraid you'll have to move into the coach section since you have a coach ticket."

To which she replied, "Listen, sir, I'm a beautiful blonde, I'm going to N.Y. and I'm sitting in first class."

After they argued for a while the first officer gave up and went to get the Captain, who said, "I'll handle this. I'm married to a beautiful blonde." So the Captain went right up to her, whispered in her ear, after which she got right up and moved into the coach section.

Both the flight attendant and first officer were shocked. The first officer asked the Captain, "I don't get it, sir. What did you say to make her move back to coach."

To which the Captain said, "Oh, that was easy. I just told her first class wasn't going to N.Y."

Airline passengers can be demanding and hard to please, hence the following true story.

Miami to New York is always a tough audience. Everyone who boards the plane wants cards, kiddie books, and anything that is "free."

One passenger asked for everything that wasn't nailed down and just couldn't be placated, so when the meals were served, it wasn't a surprise that he tugged on the flight attendant's apron while she was serving coffee with the following complaint.

Passenger: "Miss, Oh, Miss. This steak. It's such a bad steak. I can't eat this steak. I've never had such a bad steak."

Flight attendant: "I'm sorry, sir, let me see if I can take care of that steak for you."

The flight attendant put her coffee pot and tray on the floor, picked up the steak from the passenger's plate and proceeded to spank it while saying, "Bad steak, bad steak!" She put the steak back on the stunned passenger's plate and said, "I'm sure it'll behave now, sir."

She picked up her coffeepot and went on through the cabin. The bewildered passenger never said another word for the rest of the flight.

An employee for Fly-By-Night Air, who happened to have the last name of Gay, got on a plane recently using one of his company's "Free Flight" programs. However, when Mr. Gay tried to take his seat, he found it occupied by a paying passenger. So, not to make a fuss, he simply chose another seat.

Unknown to Mr. Gay, another Fly-By-Night Air flight at the airport experienced mechanical problems. The passengers of this other flight were being rerouted to various airplanes. A few were put on Mr. Gay's flight and anyone who was holding a "free" ticket was being "bumped."

Airline officials, armed with a list of these "freebie" ticket holders, boarded the plane to remove the free ticket holders. Of course, our Mr. Gay wasn't sitting in his assigned seat, as you may remember. So when the Ticket Agent approached the seat where Mr. Gay was supposed to be sitting, she asked a startled customer, "Are you Gay?"

The man shyly nodded that he was, at which point she demanded, "Then you have to get off the plane."

Our Mr. Gay, overhearing what the Ticket Agent had said, tried to clear up the situation. "You've got the wrong man. I'm Gay!" This caused an angry third passenger to yell, "Hell, I'm gay, too! You can't kick us all off!"

Confusion reigned as more and more passengers began yelling that Fly-By-Night Air had no right to remove gays from their flights.

They may still be on the tarmac fighting it out.

Passengers prefer old captains and young flight attendants.

Since I'm an infrequent flyer, I have several questions that may seem a bit naive but still cry out for answers:

Can I exchange my round-trip ticket for one that is rectangular so that it fits better on my carry-on bag?

If I fly a DC 10, can I still use my AC razor?

Isn't it dangerous to make sure the passengers are loaded before take off?

If I happened to be in the head (bathroom) when the *Fasten Seat Belt* sign comes on, can my wife do it for me?

My wife wants to know if a mudpack can be substituted for an oxygen mask?

Should I bring my own in-flight meal if I'm allergic to pretzels and peanuts?"

— Lee Murdock, Grand Forks,
North Dakota

On reaching his plane seat, a man is surprised to see a parrot strapped in next to him. He asks the flight attendant for a coffee whereupon the parrot squawks, "And get me a whiskey, you cow!" The flight attendant, flustered, brings back a whiskey for the parrot and forgets the coffee.

When this omission is pointed out to her, the parrot drains its glass and bawls, "And get me another whiskey, bitch." Quite upset, the girl comes back shaking, but with another whiskey. Still no coffee.

Unaccustomed to such slackness, the man tries the parrot's approach. "I've asked you twice for a coffee, now go get it or I'll kick your ass."

The next moment both he and the parrot have been wrenched up out of their seats and thrown out of the emergency exit by two burly stewards. Plunging downwards, the parrot turns to him and says, "For someone who can't fly, you're sure a lippy bastard!"

As the sun begins to rise, the cabin of the jetliner is suddenly illuminated. "Who turned on the f**king lights?" a male passenger, who had been sleeping since boarding, snarls at a flight attendant.

The girl had had enough of this particular character. "These are the breakfast lights, sir," she answered with forced sweetness. "The f**king lights are much dimmer. You snored right through them."

THINGS TO DO IN AN AIRPLANE

Push the flight attendant call button and pretend it gives you a shock. When you get everybody's attention, smile.

Call the Psychic Hotline from the in-flight phone and ask if they know where you are.

Drop a pen in the aisle and wait until someone reaches to help pick it up, then scream, "That's mine!"

Bring a camera and take pictures of everyone in the airplane.

Ask to the passenger next to you, "Did you feel that?"

Grimace painfully while smacking your forehead and muttering, "Shut up, all of you. Just *Shut Up!*"

Stare at another passenger for a while, then announce in horror, "You're one of *Them!*"

Listen to the airplane walls with a stethoscope.

Make explosion noises when anyone presses a flight attendant call button.

Go to the cockpit. Ask the pilot in an obnoxious voice, "Why do they call it the *Cock*pit?" Then snort as if it's the funniest thing in the world.

Ride carry-on luggage down the aisle, yelling, "Yeee-ha!"

With a desperate look, ask the flight attendant where the bathroom is, then look relieved and say, "Nevermind. Do you have any towels?"

THINGS YOU DON'T WANT TO OVERHEAR ON THE INTERCOM

"The Union President called. He said the pilots' strike starts *immediately.*"

"Hey, Pedro. What's this gismo do?"

"We'll just ask the flight attendant to wake us up when we get there."

"Hey, Jim, do you remember where we're going?"

"Buckle your seat belt. I'm going to try something I saw in a cartoon."

"Wow, we're sure a lot lighter now that we dropped that second engine!"

"Only 500 more flight hours and I'll get my license!"

"They say this plane practically flies itself. Good thing, huh?"

"*Today We Die For Allah!*"

AIRLINE PASSENGERS BILL OF RIGHTS

If a customer's flight is cancelled due to an airline pilot's sick-out, the passenger shall be entitled to see a note from that pilot's doctor.

Passengers shall always be offered a choice of either peanuts, pretzels, or a seafood platter of shrimp, scallops, oyster Rockefeller, and calamari poached and tossed with Bermuda onions, red and green peppers and balsamic vinegar with fresh pesto and drawn butter.

If a passenger requests a refund for his ticket, the passenger shall be able to obtain his refund within his lifetime.

Airlines shall be fined for forcing passengers to sit in a plane on the runway for more than an hour without providing topless dancing girls and an open bar.

Customers shall receive their checked luggage within 24 hours of their arrival. They shall also be informed at what particular flea market they can buy back the contents of their luggage.

Passengers sitting next to a crying baby will receive free alcohol and headphones.

Passengers over 400 pounds will get an aisle seat and a board to prop up their hanging buttock.

Passengers shall be given information about why a flight has been delayed, canceled, or diverted to another airport that sounds somewhat believable.

If a passenger's flight is canceled, he/she shall be given directions to the nearest bus terminal.

Passengers shall receive accurate information about their airline's frequent flyer program or at least accurate information about some other airline's frequent flyer program.

Coach passengers shall be given a foot massage from a flight attendant of their choice. First class passengers shall have the option of oral sex or a foot massage from a flight attendant of their choice.

— comedyzine.com

There was this Christian lady who had to do a lot of traveling for her business, so she did a lot of flying. But flying made her nervous, so she always took her Bible along to read. It helped relax her. One time she was sitting next to a man. When he saw her pull out her Bible, he gave a little chuckle and went back to what he was doing.

After a while he turned to her and asked, "You don't really believe all that stuff in there, do you?"

The lady replied, "Of course I do. It is the Bible."

He said, "Well, what about that guy who was swallowed by that whale?"

She replied, "Oh, Jonah. Yes, I believe that. It's in the Bible."

He asked, "Well, how do you suppose he survived all that time inside the whale?"

The lady said, "Well. I don't really know. I guess when I get to heaven, I'll ask him."

"What if he isn't in heaven?" the man asked sarcastically.

"Then you can ask him," replied the lady.

Dennis and I almost missed our honeymoon flight and were unable to get seats together. When we were airborne, I wrote my new spouse a note: To the man sitting in 16C. I find you very attractive. Would you care to join me for an unforgettable evening? The lady in 4C.

A flight attendant delivered it. A few minutes later she returned with a cocktail. The man in 16C was flattered, she told me, but said he must decline my offer since he was on his honeymoon. I was still laughing when we landed.

"Thank you for the drink," I said to my groom.

"But I didn't send you one," he replied.

He had been sitting in 14C.

Trust your captain, but keep your seat belt securely fastened anyway.

A programmer and an engineer are sitting next to each other on a long flight from LA to NY. The programmer leans over to the engineer and asks if he'd like to play a fun game. The engineer just wants to take a nap, so he politely declines and rolls over to the window to catch a few winks. The programmer persists and explains that the game is real easy and lots of fun.

He explains, "I ask you a question, and if you don't know the answer, you pay me $5. Then you ask me a question, and if I don't know the answer, I'll pay you $5." Again the engineer politely declines and tries to get to sleep.

The programmer, now somewhat agitated, says, "Okay, if you don't know the answer, you pay me $5, and if I don't know the answer, I'll pay you $50!" This catches the engineer's attention, and since he sees no end to this torment unless he plays, he agrees to the game.

The programmer asks the first question. "What's the distance from the earth to the moon?" The engineer doesn't say a word, but reaches into his wallet, pulls out a five dollar bill, and hands it to the programmer.

Now, it's the engineer's turn. He asks the programmer, "What goes up a hill with three legs and comes down on four?" The programmer looks up at him with a puzzled look. He takes out his laptop computer and searches all of his references. He taps into the Airphone with his modem and searches the net and the Library of Congress. Frustrated, he sends e-mail to his co-workers, all to no avail.

After about an hour, he wakes the engineer and hands him $50. The engineer politely takes the $50 and turns away to try to get back to sleep. The programmer, more than a little miffed, shakes the engineer and asks, "Well, so what's the answer?"

Without a word, the engineer reaches into his wallet, hands the programmer $5, and turns away to get back to sleep.

An elderly doctor and a Baptist minister were seated next to each other on the plane. The plane was delayed at the start due to some technical problems. Just after taking off, the pilot offered his apologies to the passengers and announced that a round of free drinks would be served.

When the charming air hostess came round with the trolley, the doctor ordered a gin and tonic for himself. The hostess then asked the minister whether he wanted anything.

He replied, "Oh, no! Thank you. I'd rather commit adultery than drink alcohol."

The elderly doctor promptly handed his gin and tonic back to the air-hostess said, "Madam, I didn't know there was a choice."

A shy gentleman was preparing to board a plane when he heard that the Pope was on the same flight. This is exciting, thought the gentleman. I've always been a big fan of the Pope. Perhaps I'll be able to see him in person. Imagine his surprise when the Pope sat down in the seat next to him for the flight. Still, the gentleman was too shy to speak to the Pontiff.

Shortly after takeoff, the Pope began a crossword puzzle. This is fantastic, thought the gentleman. I'm really good at crosswords. Perhaps, if the Pope gets stuck, he'll ask me for assistance.

Almost immediately, the Pope turned to the gentleman and said, "Excuse me, but do you know a four letter word referring to a woman that ends in 'unt'?"

Only one word leapt to mind. My goodness, thought the gentleman, I can't tell the Pope that. There must be another word. The gentleman thought for quite a while, then it hit him. Turning to the Pope, the gentleman said, "I think the word you're looking for is 'aunt'."

"Oooooh, of course," said the Pope. "Do you have an eraser?"

Great-aunt Bessie loved to visit her nieces and nephews. It seems she had relatives all over the country.

The problem was that, no matter how much she enjoyed seeing them, she hated flying. No matter how safe people told her it was, she was always worried that someone would have a bomb on the plane.

She read the books about how safe it was and listened to the flight attendant demonstrate all the safety features. But she still worried herself silly every time a visit was coming up.

Finally, the family decided that, maybe if she saw the statistics, she'd be convinced. So, they sent her to a friend of the family who was an actuary.

"Tell me," she said suspiciously, "What are the chances that someone will have a bomb on a plane?" The actuary looked through his tables and said, "A very small chance. Maybe one in five hundred thousand." She nodded, then thought for a moment. "So what are the odds of two people having a bomb on the same plane?"

Again he went through his tables. "Extremely remote," he said. "About one in a billion." Aunt Bessie nodded and left his office.

And from that day on, every time she flew, she took a bomb with her.

Pilot: "Folks, we've reached our cruising altitude now, so I'm going to switch the seat belt sign off. Feel free to move about as you wish, but please stay inside the plane till we land. It's a bit cold outside. If you walk on the wings, it will affect the flight pattern."

I had a job offer from a large company. They offered to fly me out to the meeting in business class. During the return flight, we were given gourmet brownies and cookies. Not hungry, I decided to save them for later, so I placed them in a vomit bag.

After the plane landed, I got up to leave. A flight attendant approached me.

She asked, "Sir, would you like for me to dispose of that for you?"

I said, "No thanks, I'm saving it for my kids."

On a cross-country flight, I tried a technique a friend had recommended for controlling fear. I asked the flight attendant for a magazine, some paper and a pencil, and proceeded to copy the words on each page of the magazine.

It was tedious, but effectively distracting. Several articles later, the attendant approached me. "I admire your thrift," she said. "But please just keep the magazine, compliments of the airline."

A man stopped one of the female flight attendants shortly after take-off and said, "I've heard the airlines will give people just about anything to keep them happy. Will you give me anything to keep me happy?"

"Of course, sir," the flight attendant cheerfully replied. "As long as it goes in a glass."

A Frenchman and an Italian were seated next to an American on an overseas flight. After a few cocktails, the men began discussing their home lives.

"Last night I made love to my wife four times," the Frenchman bragged, "and this morning she made me delicious crepes and told me how much she adored me."

"Ah, last night I made love to my wife six times," the Italian responded, "and this morning she made me a wonderful omelet and told me she could never love another man."

When the American remained silent, the Frenchman smugly asked, "And how many times did you make love to your wife last night?"

"Once," he replied.

"Only once?" the Italian arrogantly snorted. "And what did she say to you this morning?"

"Don't stop."

It was mealtime on a small airline and the flight attendant asked the passenger if he would like dinner.

"What are my choices?" he asked.

"Yes or no," she replied.

I feel compelled to add a comment made to me by a member of the cockpit crew as I departed after a very bumpy ride. He grinned and said, "You'd pay a lot of money at an amusement park for a ride like that."

Newt Gingrich is on an airplane, flying back to DC. The guy sitting next to him is immersed in a book and pays no attention to Newt. Toward the end of the flight, Newt asks, "What book is that you're reading?

Man: "It's called *Deductive Reasoning.*"

Newt: "Sounds interesting. What's it about?"

Man: "Let me give you an example."

Newt: "Okay."

Man: "Do you have a dog?"

Newt: "Yes, I do, as a matter of fact."

Man: "I would deduce from this, then, that you have a yard as well, no?"

Newt: "Yes! I do have a yard."

Man: "Then I would further deduce that you have a house next to this yard?"

Newt: "I do!"

Man: "Then I'll bet you have a family, don't you?"

Newt: "Yes, a very nice family!"

Man: "And you're a heterosexual, aren't you?"

Newt: "You betcha! I'm beginning to see how this works!"

Later that week, Newt goes out and buys the book on deductive reasoning and is determined to read it cover to cover on his return flight. His plane takes off and he begins reading.

Two hours later, the man sitting next to him notices how Newt is so engrossed in this book. He just can't keep himself from being impolite and interrupting:

Man: "Excuse me, sir, what's that you're reading?"

Newt: "It's called, *Deductive Reasoning.*"

Man: "Oh. Then you must have learned how to use deductive reasoning, eh?"

Newt: "Well, yes, as a matter of fact I have. Let me show you how it works."

Man: "Okay." Newt: "Do you have a dog?"

Man: "No."

Newt: "Well, then, you must be a homosexual!"

As the airliner pushed back from the gate, the flight attendant gave the passengers the usual information regarding seat belts, etc. Finally, she said, "Now sit back and enjoy your trip while your captain, Judith Campbell, and crew take you safely to your destination."

Joe, sitting in the eighth row, thought; "Did I hear her right? Is the captain a woman?"

When the attendants came by with the drink cart, he said, "Did I understand you right? Is the captain a woman?"

"Yes," said the attendant, "In fact, this entire crew is female."

"My God," said Joe. "I'd better have two scotch and sodas. I don't know what to think of all those women up there in the cockpit."

"That's another thing," said the attendant. "We no longer call it the *cockpit.* Now it's the *box office.*"

The rich-and-famous don't always succeed in flaunting the rules, as the world boxing champion learned on one flight. While the aircraft was being pushed back, the flight attendant asked him to buckle his seatbelt.

The champ replied, "Superman don't need no seatbelt!"

Without missing a beat, the savvy flight attendant replied: "Superman don't need no airplane, either!"

The boxer buckled up without another word.

Heard onboard a Southwest Airlines flight during the safety information speech: "Today, our flight will be passing over 2,537 hot tubs, 1,096 pools, and 537 private ponds, so here is the water evacuation information.

On a flight to Chicago, a gentleman had made several attempts to get into the men's restroom, but it was always occupied. The flight attendant noticed his predicament. "Sir," she said, "You may use the ladies room if you promise not to touch any of the buttons on the wall."

He did what he needed to, and as he sat there he noticed the buttons he had promised not to touch. Each button was identified by letters: WW, WA, PP, and a red one labeled ATR.

Who would know if he touched them? He couldn't resist. He pushed WW. Warm water was sprayed gently upon his bottom. What a nice feeling, he thought. Men's restrooms don't have nice things like this.

Anticipating greater pleasure, he pushed the WA button. Warm air replaced the warm water, gently drying his underside. When this stopped, he pushed the PP button. A large powder puff caressed his bottom, adding a fragile scent of spring flowers to this unbelievable pleasure.

The ladies restroom was more than a restroom; it was tender, loving pleasure. When the powder puff completed its job, he couldn't wait to push the ATR button, which he knew would be supreme ecstasy.

The next thing he knew he was in a hospital. A nurse was staring down at him with a smirk on her face. "What happened?" he exclaimed.

"You pushed one too many buttons," replied the nurse. The last button marked ATR was an Automatic Tampon Remover. Your privates are under your pillow."

While sitting in the upper deck business class front seat of a Cathay Pacific 747 in Taipei, the following announcement was heard over the cabin PA system:

"Ladies and gentlemen, we're overbooked and are offering anyone $1,000 plus a seat on the next flight in exchange for their seat on this flight."

After a short pause, someone in the cockpit loudly accepted the offer.

A man is flying from Los Angeles to New York. During the meal service, he accidentally knocked the spoon off to the aisle with his elbow. The flight attendant immediately took a spoon from his pocket and placed it on his tray table. The man was impressed by the promptness of the service and asked, "Do all flight attendants carry a spoon in their pockets?"

The flight attendant answered, "We had an efficiency expert evaluate our operation. He determined that 25% of our customers knock the spoon off their tray tables. By carrying a spare spoon, we all save trips to the galley and can be much more efficient."

Later, as the flight attendant is picking his dirty tray up, the customer asked, "Excuse me for asking, but why do you have a string hanging from your fly?"

The flight attendant replied, "The efficiency expert determined that we were spending too much time washing our hands after we went to the bathroom. To counteract this, we tie strings to our penises."

The customer looked confused. "How does that help?" he asked.

"Well, when I go to the bathroom, I just use the string. Since I never touched myself, I don't need to wash my hands."

The customer nodded and asked, "But how do you get it back in your pants?"

The flight attendant smiled. "I don't know about the other guys, but I use the spoon."

There may be fifty ways to leave your lover, but there are only four ways out of this airplane.

WHY?

The person in the middle seat gets both arm rests.

If you must work on your flight, you'll experience turbulence as soon as you touch fingers to laptop.

Only passengers seated in window seats ever have to go to the lavatory.

The crying baby on board your flight is always seated next to you.

The best-looking woman on your flight is never seated next to you.

The strength of the turbulence is directly proportional to the temperature of your coffee.

— Gunter's *Second Law of Air Travel*

I was flying across the Atlantic one Christmas on a Greek Charter plane back when ticket prices were low and airplanes were full. It had been a long day, including battling the seas of humanity crowding through the airport, but we had finally boarded the aging DC 8.

The passengers were in a restless, though festive mood. The cabin attendants were rushing around trying to get us all calmed down so the flight could begin.

One attendant spotted a bag on the floor and said, "I'm sorry, sir, but this row is an emergency exit. You'll have to put the bag under the seat in front of you."

After a few moments, she bustled back, saw the bag was still visible and in a strained voice said, "I'm sorry sir, but this is an emergency exit, so please move the bag out of the way." and hurried off again.

On her next trip the bag was still visible on the floor and she snapped, "You're going to have to move this bag. It's blocking an emergency exit" to which a disembodied voice behind me replied, "Why? Are you expecting this airplane to crash?"

— Liam Gartside, tgartside@mcimail.com

Several years ago, Australian Airlines (later to become Qantas Domestic) used a barf bag that doubled, presumably as an alternate, *not* additional use, as a film-mailing envelope for a large photo processing company.

This colourfully printed barf bag encouraged passengers to, and I swear I'm not making this up, "Re-live those wonderful memories."

Taking advantage of the classic Midwest winter, solid overcast with about a 2,000 ceiling, one local resident on the approach path to Milwaukee Mitchell Airport's runway 19R (right) last year offered a neatly lettered rooftop sign, *Welcome to Cleveland!*

On a flight from London to Vancouver a few years ago on a 747, I overheard this conversation. A gentleman, obviously a first-time flyer, was nervously asking the grandmother beside him about the length of the flight, etc.

After take-off, he fell completely silent and fixed his stare on the inboard engine, apparently waiting for it to drop off.

After about half an hour, the grandmother tapped him on the shoulder and said, "Son, if you'd like to go to the washroom, I'll watch it for you."

— John Reynolds, reynolds@oberon.ark.com

A man boards an airplane and takes his seat. As he settles in, he glances up and sees a very beautiful woman boarding the plane. He soon realizes she's heading straight toward his seat. Lo and behold, she takes the seat right beside his.

Eager to strike up a conversation, he blurts out, "Business trip or vacation?"

She turns, smiles, and says, "Business. I'm going to the annual nymphomaniac convention in Chicago."

He swallows hard. Here's the most gorgeous woman he's ever seen, sitting next to him, and she's going to a meeting of nymphomaniacs! Struggling to maintain his composure, he calmly asks, "What's your business role at this convention?"

"Lecturer," she says. "I use my experience to debunk some of the popular myths about sexuality."

"Really," he says, swallowing hard, "What myths are those?"

"Well," she explains, "One popular myth is that African American men are the most well- endowed. In fact, it's the Native American Indian who's most likely to possess that trait. Another popular myth is that French men are the best lovers, when actually it's the men of Jewish descent. However, we've found that the best potential lover in all categories is the Southern Redneck."

Suddenly, the woman becomes a little uncomfortable and blushes. "I'm sorry," she says, "I shouldn't be discussing this with you. I don't even know your name!"

"Tonto!" the man says. "Tonto Goldstein, but my friends call me, Bubba."

"I've never flown before," said the nervous old lady to the pilot. "You'll bring me down safely, won't you?"

"All I can say, ma'am," said the pilot, "is that I've never left anyone up there yet!"

According to *The Australian,* an airliner recently encountered severe vibration in flight. The captain decided to make an emergency landing and switched on the seat belt sign. The vibration stopped immediately.

A passenger emerged from a lavatory and explained that he had been jogging in place inside.

Before going on his first plane journey, a man was told that chewing gum would stop his ears popping during the flight. As they landed, the man turned to his friend and said, "The chewing gum works fine, but how do I get it out of my ears?"

Two blondes were flying to Miami from Cleveland. Fifteen minutes into the flight, the captain announced, "One of the engines has failed, and the flight will be an hour longer. But don't worry, we have three engines left."

Thirty minutes later, the captain announced, "One more engine has failed. The flight will be two hours longer. But don't worry, we have two engines left."

An hour later the captain announced, "One more engine has failed, and the flight will be three hours longer. But don't worry, we have one engine left."

One blonde looked at the other and said, "If we lose one more engine, we'll be up here all day."

Ever wonder why they never show the film *Alive* in-flight? It's not because of the film's content. It's because the people in the film are eating better than the people on board.

Attendant: "Welcome aboard Ala Carte Air, sir. May I see your ticket?"

Passenger: "Sure."

Attendant: "You're in seat 12B. That will be $5, please."

Passenger: "What for?"

Attendant: "For telling you where to sit."

Passenger: "But I already knew where to sit."

Attendant: "Nevertheless, we're now charging a seat locator fee of $5. It's the airline's new policy."

Passenger: "That's the craziest thing I ever heard. I won't pay it."

Attendant: "Sir, do you want a seat on this flight or not?"

Passenger: "Yes, yes. All right, I'll pay. But the airline is going to hear about this."

Attendant: "Thank you. My goodness, your carry-on bag looks heavy. Would you like me to stow it in the overhead compartment for you?"

Passenger: "That would be swell, thanks."

Attendant: "No problem. Up we go, and done! That'll be $10, please."

Passenger: "What?"

Attendant: "The airline now charges a $10 carry-on assistance fee."

Passenger: "This is extortion. I won't stand for it."

Attendant: "Actually, you're right, you can't stand. You need to sit and fasten your seat belt. We're about to push back from the gate. But first I need that $10."

Passenger: "No way!"

Attendant: "Sir, if you don't comply, I'll be forced to call the air marshal. And you really don't want me to do that."

Passenger: "Why not? Is he going to shoot me?"

Attendant: "No, but there's a $50 air-marshal hailing fee."

Passenger: "Oh, all right, here, take the $10. I can't believe this."

Attendant: "Thank you for your cooperation, sir. Is there anything else I can do for you?"

Passenger: "Yes. It's stuffy in here, and my overhead fan doesn't seem to work. Can you fix it?"

Attendant: "Your overhead fan isn't broken, sir. Just insert two quarters into the overhead coin slot for the first five minutes."

Passenger: "The airline is charging me for cabin air?"

Attendant: "Of course not, sir. Stagnant cabin air is provided free of charge. It's the circulating air that costs fifty cents."

Passenger: "I don't have any quarters. Can you make change for a dollar?"

Attendant: "Certainly, sir! Here you go!"

Passenger: "But you've given me only three quarters for my dollar!"

Attendant: "Yes, there's a change making fee of 25 cents."

Passenger: "For cryin' out loud. All I have left is a lousy quarter! What the heck can I do with this?"

Attendant: "Hang onto it. You'll need it later for the lavatory."

With increased air travel during the holiday season, many are winging long distances for the first time since last holiday season. For the infrequent traveler, I've kept a log of my last cross-country flight to explain just how bad it can be. The flight was from Los Angeles (LAX) to New York City (JFK).

4:30 a.m.: Picked up at home by Phil's Speedy Discount Airport Shuttle. Motto: "If we're more than fifteen minutes late, we wouldn't be the least bit surprised."

5:45: Arrive Los Angeles International Airport. Curbside check-in offers hi-tech Computerized Tracking System (CTS) which ensures that your luggage will arrive in Nepal twenty minutes before you land in New York.

6:00: Ticket counter uses new Random Queuing System (RQS). Queue is a British term meaning: "You're in the wrong line, stupid." I queue up in the Odd Size line, then am booted out when told Odd Size refers to luggage only.

6:15: Security check. Foreign passenger ahead of me is asked, "Did person or persons unknown to you pack your luggage, pat your butt, or recite lyrics to anything by Puff Daddy?"

7:30: Pre-boarding begins for pre-boards who need assistance, assistants who need pre-boarding, first class, business class, no class, private first classes, tattooed youths, passengers on the wrong plane and those who play dumb and pretend their row has been called.

8:15: Pilot announces, "The fine folks in maintenance have informed me they have to recalibrate and functionalize the leading edge hydraulic spoiler actuation pressure stabilizer and will get on it as soon as Chief Mechanic, Fat Mel, finishes his doughnut."

11:46: Takeoff.

11:47: Emergency landing to remove Fat Mel from engine cowling.

12:15 p.m.: Re-takeoff.

12:45: Breakfast. Choices are runny eggs with something green in them or Fruit Loops and curdled milk.

1:15: Aisle-racing by sugar-rushed toddlers begins.

1:45: Pilot asks if anyone has seen his keys to the liquor cabinet.

2:00: Edited for airline version of *Showgirls* begins.

2:06: Edited for airline version of *Showgirls* ends.

3:15: Pilot says, "Passengers on our left side can see Columbus, OH. Those on the right can see Lima, Peru."

4:45: Surly flight attendants collect the breakfast trays.

5:00: Inadvertently land at Teterboro, NJ, airport long-term parking lot. Pilot says he'll taxi aircraft to JFK.

5:15: Skippy, the co-pilot, collects spare change for turnpike tolls.

5:30: Detour to Hackensack so Skippy can drop off laundry and tuck in the kids.

6:15: Arrive at gate.

6:45: Computerized Tracking System claims I don't have any luggage, I never had luggage, I'll never have luggage again, and it's not that fond of my tie.

7:45: Take cab driven by man whose name has seventeen consonants and an umlaut. Ululates show tunes all the way to the hotel.

11:45: Luggage from previous trip delivered to room.

— by John H. Corcoran, Jr.

CHILDREN

A little boy and his mother were taking his first commercial airplane ride. After boarding the plane, taking off, and being at cruise altitude for some time, the puzzled boy looked at his mother and said, "So when do we get smaller?"

A pilot was flying in his C (Cessna)-205 with his two sons, ages four and six, over the mountains of Tennessee, bucking a strong headwind. He looked in the back and noticed the boys looking down in the valley below, where a train was also heading northwest, and they were barely gaining on it. Nothing was said.

Four months later, the younger son, Brian, was called to kindergarten roundup, where the officious school psychologist was conducting evaluations. When Brian's turn came, the shrink said, "Brian, what color is an apple?"

Brian replied, "Are you talking about the inside or the outside of the apple?"

Perplexed, the shrink went on, "Well, Brian, which goes faster, a train or a plane?"

Brian replied, "Well, Doctor, it kind of depends on the headwinds."

A new mother boarded the aircraft with her little infant. Proudly making her way to her seat and settling in, she uncovers the infant's head. The passenger seated next to her said, "Lady, that's the ugliest baby I've ever seen. *It looks just like a monkey!*"

The new mother became extremely upset and started crying. The flight attendant heard the lady crying and walked over to console her.

Flight Attendant: "Ma'am, may I get something for you? Coffee, tea, milk or a banana for your monkey?"
— Brenda Moss-Clifton, brendamc@bws.com

An airline pilot was traveling with his young son aboard a company jet. Late into the flight, the son said, "Dad, I can tell we're getting ready to land."

The father proudly started thinking, he must have noticed the attitude of the aircraft changing, or maybe he heard the flaps extending and felt the speed brakes rumbling.

When he asked his son how he knew they were about to land, the reply was, "Because the flight attendants are putting on their high-heels."

On a penny-a-pound ride I once gave at an airport open house, I used a 1957 Cessna 172. The one with the flap handle on the floor. On short final approach, I pulled on all forty degrees of flap, but we still floated somewhat.

Later, my young passenger told his mother that he liked the flight but, "When the guy pulled the emergency brake on, we still didn't stop!"

I was working on a transcontinental flight when a young child who was traveling with his mother became irritable and started to cry. A businessman, who was trying to catch up on his paperwork pled with me to do something about the child's behavior. I had no clue.

The mother and the flight attendants tried to quiet the child with toys and cookies, without success. Then a man approached the mother and offered to help. In desperation, she agreed. He immediately started to make funny faces and noises. The child gradually ceased to cry and responded happily to the man's expressions.

The mother sighed with relief, thanked the man, and asked if he had children of his own. "I'm not married," he replied. After a moment he said, "I'm a baby photographer."

We had just completed a flight in a commercial airliner from Chicago to Cedar Rapids, IA. The aircraft had taxied to the gate and the engines shut down. Everyone in the now-quiet aircraft was waiting for the seatbelt light to extinguish when my four-year-old brother's voice called out, "But, Dad! We didn't drop any bombs!"

During the descent of a flight to Florida, my eighteen-month-old son's ears began to bother him. I handed him a baby bottle of water saying, "This will make your ears feel better." He looked uncomprehendingly at the bottle, then at me, then back to the bottle. With a shrug, exhibiting total trust in his mother, he lifted the bottle and stuck the nipple right into his ear!

— Dana Dunlevy, Florham Park, New Jersey

SIX

Flight Attendants

SO YOU WANT TO BE A FLIGHT ATTENDANT

First, fill several large boxes with rocks. Lift them over your head and place them on the top shelf of a closet. Slam the door shut until the boxes fit. Do this until you feel a disk slip in your back. Smile.

Turn on a radio. Be sure to set it between stations so there is plenty of static. Turn on the vacuum cleaner and garbage disposal. Run them all night. Smile.

Remove the covers from several TV entrees. Place them in a hot oven. Leave the food in the oven until it's completely dried out. Remove the hot trays with your bare hands. Serve to your family. Don't include anything for yourself. Eat peanuts. Smile.

Serve your family a beverage one hour after they've received their meal. Make them remain in their seats during this time. Ask them to scream at you and complain about the service. Eat peanuts. Smile.

Scrounge uneaten rolls off the plates to eat two hours later when you're really hungry. Eat peanuts. Smile.

Place a straight-backed chair in a closet next to a bathroom, facing a blank wall. Use a belt to strap yourself into it. Eat the stale rolls you saved from your family's meal, preferably while someone is *using* the bathroom. Smile.

Ask your family to use the bathroom as frequently as possible. Tell them to make splashing water a game and see who can leave the most disgusting mess. Clean the bathroom every hour throughout the night. Drink stale coffee in the closet next to the bathroom. Eat peanuts. Smile.

Make a narrow aisle between several dining room chairs and randomly scatter your husband's wing-tips and loafers along the way. Turn off the lights and spend the night walking up and down the aisle while banging your shins against the chair legs and tripping over the shoes. Drink several cups of cold, stale coffee to keep yourself awake. Eat peanuts. Smile.

Stay up all night, then wake your family in the morning and serve them a cold, hard sweet roll. Don't forget to smile and wish them a nice day when they leave for work and school. Ask them to berate you. Eat peanuts. Smile.

After the family leaves, take a suitcase and go out (preferably in winter) in the yard. If it's not raining, turn on the sprinkling system and stand in the cold and the wet for thirty minutes, pretending you're waiting for the crew bus to pick you up. Then go inside and wait by your bedroom door for *another* thirty minutes while an imaginary maid cleans and makes up your room. Smile.

Change into street clothes and shop for five hours. Pick up carry-out food from a local deli. Go back home. Sit on your bed and eat your meal. Set your alarm for 3 a.m. so you'll be ready for your wake-up call. (It's now 12:30 a.m.) Eat peanuts. Smile.

Repeat the above schedule for four days in a row, and you'll be ready to work your first trip as a flight attendant!

Repeat the above schedule after three days off, every week for twelve month's straight. *Now* you're ready to *Be* a flight attendant!

TIPS FOR ASPIRING FLIGHT ATTENDANTS:

Oven mitts help create the illusion of hot meals.

Effective nut distribution is the key to happy passengers.

Excessive fingernail length is the primary cause of beverage spillage.

Fashion hint: practice scarf arrangements.

Don't attempt to dispense spiritual or psychological advice.

Remember, you're a waitress on fast-moving vehicle!

Q: What separates flight attendants from the scum of the earth?

A: The cockpit door!

From a Southwest Airlines flight attendant:

"Welcome aboard Southwest Flight 123. To operate your seatbelt, insert the metal tab into the buckle and pull tight. It works just like every other seatbelt. If you don't know how to operate one, you probably shouldn't be out in public unsupervised. In the event of a sudden loss of cabin pressure, oxygen masks will descend from the ceiling. Stop screaming, grab the mask and pull it over your face. If you have a small child traveling with you, secure your mask before assisting with theirs. If you're traveling with two small children, decide which one you love the most."

Southwest Airlines FA: (said in a low, slow, monotone, by a male flight attendant) "Pushing the button with the picture of the light bulb turns the light on. Pushing the button with the picture of the flight attendant [pause] does not turn us on."

The Captain said, "I'm retiring next month and wish to pass something on to young pilots who'll be flying this airline after I'm gone."

His co-pilot leaned an attentive ear toward his gray-haired Captain in anticipation of some unwritten rule-of-thumb or some secret technique for ensuring smooth landings.

The Captain confided, "In thirty years of flying the line, if there's anything I've learned, its this: the smaller the flight attendant, the heavier her suitcase, the harder she slams the cockpit door."

"Good morning, everyone, and welcome aboard American Trans Air flight 458. Before we take off, I'd like to call your attention to some safety features we have on board. Each seat on board comes with a safety information card. We'd like you to read carefully in preparation for the mid-flight test later on.

I'd also like to call your attention to the smartly dressed flight attendants standing before you, who will be pointing out exits and other aircraft equipment. There are six exits on board, two at the back, two in the middle, and two at the front. Should there be a sudden loss of cabin pressure; oxygen masks will automatically drop from above. Place these over your mouth and nose and begin breathing normally. Adults, put your own mask on before helping a child or an adult who's acting like a child.

Once we've reached a comfortable altitude, the captain will turn off the seat belt sign. You'll be free to move about the cabin. If you need to use the bathroom, we have six on board, three forward and three aft. If you're unfamiliar with the terms 'fore' and 'aft,' you're in some trouble, aren't you?

We'd like to remind you that this is a no-smoking flight and, to ensure this, smoke detectors are installed in all lavatories. Federal law prohibits tampering with this device or with the hidden camera. Photographs will be available at the end of the flight.

For the moment, sit back, relax, and enjoy the flight as I and the rest of the cabin attendants go below deck to begin searching through your luggage."

Q: What's the difference between a flight attendant and a jet engine?

A: The jet engine stops whining at the gate.

Q: An airhead flight attendant, a smart flight attendant, and Santa Claus jumped off the airplane after they lost both engines. Who made the largest splash?

A: The airhead flight attendant. The others don't exist.

Q: What do you call a bunch of senior flight attendants in a spa?

A: Gorillas in the mist.

Q: What's the best way to get a flight attendant into bed?

A: Make them work five legs back to back and an all-nighter.

Q: How do you make a flight attendant come with one finger?

A: Pressing the flight attendant call button.

Q: How do you recognize a flight attendant at a party?

A: They're the only ones eating standing up and cleaning their hands with the curtains.

Q: How does a flight attendant tell a passenger to go to hell?

A: "I'll be right back!"

Q: What do you call a pregnant flight attendant?
A: Pilot Error.

Q. What do you call a bunch of flight attendants in a basement?
A. A Whine Cellar!

Q: How many flight attendants does it take to change a light bulb?
A: One hundred. One to actually change it. Ninety-nine to bitch about it.

The plane's cabin was being served by an obviously homosexual flight attendant who was just as obviously enjoying himself.

He came swishing down the aisle and said to a man and the woman seated beside him, "Captain Marvey has asked me to announce that he'll be landing the big scary plane shortly, lovely people, so if you could just put up your trays that would be super."

On his trip back up the aisle, he noticed that the woman hadn't moved a muscle. "Perhaps you didn't hear me over those big-brute engines. I asked you to raise your trazy-poo so the main man can pitty-pat us on the ground."

She calmly turned her head and said, "In my country, I'm called a Princess. I take orders from no one!"

"Well, sweet-cheeks, in my country, I'm called a Queen, so I outrank you. Now put up the tray, bitch!"

— Xenia

Flight attendant placing a drink order: "Okay, the man in 12 C wants a soda, and we need three martinis for the cockpit."

What's the difference between a teacher, a nurse, and a flight attendant in bed?

The teacher will tell you, "I'm gonna teach you how to do it, Then we'll go over and over it until we get it right."

The nurse will say, "I'm gonna do it slowly and I promise it's not going to hurt."

And the flight attendant will tell you, "Put it over your nose and mouth and continue to breathe normally."

On a nice little De Havilland twin prop, Toronto to Baltimore: "Okay, so we have fifteen of you today. Anyone not flown before?

Excellent. No virgins. Then I'll do the short version.

Exits over the wings, life jackets beneath the seats, oxygen masks drop out of the ceiling. Seats up, belts on, read the cards, and enjoy your flight.

Questions?"

After a passenger continuously pressed the flight attendant Call Button, demanding attention and complaining about the service, the flight attendant says, "We're here to *save* your ass, not to *kiss* it."

Flying to Los Angeles from San Francisco, a passenger noticed that, although the flight was a particularly smooth one, the *Fasten Seat Belts* sign stayed illuminated throughout the entire trip. Just before landing, he asked the flight attendant about it.

"Well," she explained, "Up front there are seventeen University of California girls going to Los Angeles for the weekend. In back, there are 25 Coast Guard enlistees. What would you have us do?"

Coming back from Vegas to Austin on Southwest Airlines, the 737 was for the most part filled with business-type suit and tie guys. We were all getting settled, digging for magazines, pulling out laptops, joking, chatting, etc. when the flight attendant announced over the intercom, "Did anyone lose a brown wallet?"

All talking and all commotion instantly ceased as hands instinctively went for back pockets and eyes went forward to where she was standing in the cabin, which was now completely silent.

She continued, "Now that I have your attention, I'd like to point out the emergency exits located on either side of the aircraft…"

HOW TO MAKE A FLIGHT ATTENDANT GO CRAZY:

Wait until they've hauled the meal and beverage carts up the aisle, then get in between the carts and attempt to walk to the lavatory.

Wear your headphones on super high volume. Ignore the flight attendant with the beverage cart, then jump like they've surprised you. When you do finally look at them, scream, "I can't hear you!" at the top of your lungs.

Press the flight attendant call button at least four times, then turn the call light off so they can't find you.

Ask for coffee. When the flight attendant comes back, ask for milk. When she returns, ask for sugar.

On aircraft with no video equipment, ask when the movie starts.

During the beverage service, ask for a frozen Piña Colada.

Ask for Espresso Coffee.

Eat a banana and hand the peelings to the flight attendant.

Hand your baby's diaper to the flight attendant.

When you get an exit row seat, ask the flight attendant, "I'll be the first one out, won't I? Or do we get free drinks for sitting here?"

— submitted by Rege737

When the flight attendant briefs you on the exit operation, ask her, "Can I practice now?"

— submitted by Rege737

"As we prepare for takeoff, please make sure your tray tables and seat backs are fully upright in their most uncomfortable position."

SEVEN

Airports

"Terminals have always been, and probably always will be, the "bottle-necks" of transportation, whether of ground, water, or air systems."

— Harry H. Blee, 1932

"That is the trouble with flying: We always have to return to airports. Think of how much fun flying would be if we didn't have to return."

— Henry Minizburg, *Why I Hate Flying*

"If God had really intended men to fly, He'd make it easier to get to the airport."

— George Winters

The only thing that scares me about flying is the drive to the airport.

AIRPORT TIPS

Worried about parking at the airport? Just park right in front of the airport. Sure, your car will be towed, but if you're gone for more than a few days, it will cost you about the same as airport parking. And it's *really* convenient.

If you need to smuggle something through security, always purchase a flight attendant's uniform and carry-on bag at your local uniform store. Dressed as a flight attendant, you can quickly pass through airport security. An extra bonus is you also get better meals on the flight. You might even get a date with a man. Heterosexual men should keep this in mind before buying the uniform.

Almost 150 years ago, President Lincoln found it necessary to hire a private investigator, Alan Pinkerton, for protection. That was the beginning of the Secret Service. Since that time, federal police authority has grown to a large number of multi-letter agencies, FBI, CIA, INS, IRS, DEA, BATF, ICE, etc.

Now comes the "Federal Air Transportation Airport Security Service."

Can't you see them now, these highly trained men and women in their black outfits with their initials in large white letters across their backs: "FATASS."

I feel safer already.

Feel free to leave your bags unattended or with strangers. After all, we must all learn to trust one another.

When travel plans go awry, you need a sense of humor, along with the ability to entertain yourself. Always bring along a book, game, or other form of amusement such as a blow up doll or some other sexual toy to keep yourself occupied. And don't forget some wet wipes for an easy clean up.

For a little fun, ask someone if he/she will carry your attaché case through the metal detector. For extra enjoyment, use a camcorder to record their responses. This is a great way to pass time as you wait for your flight.

Another great way to pass time at the airport is to go to the arrival gate and greet strangers as they deplane. Shake the hand of a stranger while asking, "Good to see you. How have you been?" This will cause them great anxiety while they try and remember your name, particularly if you run up to a woman while her husband waits or if you're woman who runs up to a man. If you really have chutzpuh and are a man, run up to another man and give him a big hug and kiss.

The laughs may be plentiful or you may get punched. This is an enjoyable way to kill time while in an airport, particularly if you like kissing strangers.

When traveling, always wear a back brace or support. This way, when someone is picking you up, they'll see your back support and pick your bags up for you. Having someone else pick up your heavy luggage is smart.

If flying is so safe, why do they call the airport the terminal?

The shorter the flight or the tighter the connection, the farther away the gate.

When the flight information monitors show that 1/3 of the flights are canceled and 1/3 are delayed, they're lying about the other 1/3.

The later in the evening your flight arrives or departs, the more distant the gate you're assigned (even though there are lots of empty gates closer).

Did you ever try to find a power outlet for your computer in a gate area?

Don't stay at an airport hotel at an air freight hub.

There are no newly built Days Inns. They were all something else before.

Never stay in a hotel that's called "historic."

Never stay in a hotel that nails the TV remote control or the radio/alarm clock to the table.

The most sensitive mechanism in modern aviation is the shower control in a layover hotel.

YOU KNOW YOU'RE RUNNING LATE WHEN:
The FedEx planes have departed.
The hotel shuttle buses have stopped running.
The arrival monitors only show your flight and the departure monitors are blank or show departures at 6:15 AM tomorrow.
The concession stands are closed, but tomorrow's newspapers have been dropped off.
You're the only passenger on the rental car shuttle bus.
The only folks at the airport are the cleaning crews with vacuum cleaners or scrubbing machines.

YOU KNOW YOU'RE AT A SMALL AIRPORT WHEN:
They have good food.
The crops grow within 100 feet of the runway.
Flight info is hand-written on a white board.

The gate agent doesn't know where the destination is.

The car rental counter is closed when you arrive but the keys are left waiting on the counter.

You and the flight attendant are the only passengers.

Flight altitude is 1500 feet and flight time is ten minutes.

The parking lot is $2/day and on the honor system.

The luggage is hand-searched. There are no metal detectors.

The pilot leaves the right engine running when you get on or off.

Only one runway is plowed for the winter.

The landing lights are kerosene smudge pots.

There are more doors than passengers on the plane.

You volunteer to be bumped, and they put you in a taxi to your destination.

The snowmobiles on the street keep you awake all night.

When you scan the radio dial and don't find a station.

Always turn the radio down before turning the key in a rental car.

SIGNS YOU'RE IN AN UNSAFE AIRPORT

Machines sell insurance just for your time in the airport.

The ground crew is bringing jet fuel to the plane in their cupped hands.

Runways have passing lanes.

Cheering crowd has gathered in the lounge surrounding a pilot doing shots of Stoli.

RULES

Actual laws from a variety of places in The United States. Excerpts from Private Pilot, November 1987 (reposted by a Frequent Flyer).

It is against the law for a pilot to tickle a female flying student under her chin with a feather duster to get her attention. - Columbia, PA

It is a violation for a woman over 200 pounds and attired in shorts to pilot or ride in an airplane. - Pocataligo, GA

Lingerie can't be hung on a clothesline at the airport unless the undies are carefully hidden from prying eyes by a "suitable screen." - Kidderville, NH

No female shall appear in a bathing suit at any airport in this state unless she is escorted by two officers or is armed with a club. The provisions of this statute shall not apply to females weighing less than 90 pounds nor exceeding 200 pounds. - KY

It is a violation of local law for any pilot or passenger to carry an ice cream cone in his/her pocket while either flying or waiting to board a plane. - Lowes Crossroads, DE

Pilots and passengers are prohibited from eating onions between the hours of 7 AM and 7 PM. - Bluff, UT

Citizens are not allowed to enter an airplane within four hours of eating garlic. - Wakefield, RI

No female wearing a nightgown can be taken for a flight on a private plane. - Headland, AL

It is against the law to eat ice cream in the local airport with a fork. - Bicknell, IN

No married man can go flying on Sunday. - Burdoville, VT

No married man can go flying without his spouse along at any time, unless he has been married for more than twelve months. - West Union, OH

No one can play cards on the airport grounds with a woman, a child, or an Indian. - White Horse, NM

No one; man, woman or child, can be seen flying while barefoot. - Fairplay, CO

Don't let your horse fall asleep in the airport. - Peewee, WV

Women who are single, widowed, or divorced are banned from parachuting on Sunday. - Crawford, NE

No turtle races shall be held at the airport. - Bourbon, MS

People cannot play checkers at the airport, 'lest they acquire a taste for gambling'. - Clearbrook, MN

Citizens cannot carry a slingshot on an airplane without special permission. - Okanogan, WA

No pilot can eat unshelled roasted peanuts or watermelon while flying. - Leadwood, MO

No person is allowed to read the Sunday paper while sitting in a chair at the airport while church services are going on. - Upperville, VA

No flyer may wear a pair of pants with hip pockets while flying. - Guyman, OK

Gargling is prohibited while flying. - Hackberry, AZ

Loud burping while walking around the airport is prohibited. - Halstead, KS

It is against the law to sneeze in an airplane. - Lynch Heights, DE

No flying instructor may place his arm around a woman without a good and lawful reason (while flying). - Rock Springs, WY

Juggling in front of an airplane is illegal. - Wellsboro, PA

Roosters may crow, only if it is done at least 300 feet from the airport. - Stugis, MI

Like a lot of pilots I know, I tend to read back confirmation and reservation numbers and, out of habit, use the phonetic pronunciations for all alphabetic characters. Recently, while dealing with a car rental company, I was reading back my confirmation number: One Five Alpha Two Quebec, when I was interrupted with "Is that with a C or a K?"

I'm boldly sitting in a commercial airplane, and I'm cool as a cucumber. This is because we're on the ground at the famous Atlanta airport, which means we'll all be dead from starvation long before we take off, and because there are 1,450 aircraft ahead of us, including a number of biplanes still awaiting clearance to participate in World War I.

EIGHT

Airlines

FLY-BY-NIGHT AIRWAYS ADVERTISING SLOGANS:

When you just can't wait for the world to come to you.

We're Amtrak with wings.

Join our frequent near-miss program.

On certain flights, every section is a smoking section.

Ask about our out-of-court settlements.

Noisy engines? We'll turn 'em off!

Our staff has lots of experience consoling next-of-kin.

Complimentary champagne during free-fall.

Enjoy the in-flight movie in the plane next to you.

The kids will love our inflatable slides.

You think it's so easy, get your own damn plane!

Which will fall faster, our stock price or our planes?

Our pilots are all terminally ill and have nothing to lose.

We may be landing on your street.

Terrorists are afraid to fly with us.

Bring a bathing suit.

Some airlines are content to fly thousands of feet over landmarks. We try to get as close as possible for the best view.

Find out if there really is a God.

A real man lands where he wants to.

We never make the same mistake twice.

— Lederman

GREAT AIRLINE LIES

Short hold for a gate.
Short hold for air traffic control.
Short wait for a mechanic (or a part).
Brief holding pattern.
Slight delay.
Light turbulence.
Momentary re-boarding.

TEN SIGNS YOU'VE CHOSEN THE WRONG AIRLINE:

Ground crew seen using pennies to check tire wear.

Trendy desert-pastel paint job upon closer inspection turns out to be primer-yellow and Bondo[1]-pink.

Man with oily rag hanging from the back pocket of his dirty overalls turns out to be the pilot.

Voice on P.A. system warns you to keep your hands and arms inside the aircraft while it's in motion.

Flight attendant offers coffee, tea, or Valium.

Air sickness bags printed with the Lord's Prayer.

Suspicious-looking passenger in the next seat over is nervously counting down minutes.

Pilot asks if anyone on board has jumper cables with them.

A telephone with a really long cord attaches the flight crew with the control tower.

Navigator keeps asking, "Are we there yet?"

Passengers on a Lufthansa flight heard this announcement from the captain: "Ladies and gentlemen, I am sorry to inform

---

1 Body putty

you that we've lost power to all of our engines and will shortly crash into the ocean."

The passengers were obviously worried about this situation, but were somewhat comforted by the captain's next announcement. "Ladies and gentlemen, we at Lufthansa have prepared for such an emergency, and we would now like you to rearrange your seating so that all the non-swimmers are on the left side of the plane and all the swimmers are on the right side of the plane."

After this announcement all the passengers rearranged their seating to comply with the captain's request. Two minutes later the captain made a belly landing in the ocean. The captain once again made an announcement: "Ladies and gentlemen, we've crashed into the ocean. All of the swimmers on the right side of the plane, open your emergency exits and quickly swim away from the plane. For all of the non-swimmers on the left side of plane.... Thank you for flying Lufthansa!"

Two Eastern pilots are looking at the little safety card from the barf-bag pocket. They are *laughing* at it.

The fellow next to them asks what's so funny. They point to the diagram of the plane floating perkily on top of the water, like a giant inflatable pool toy, while the passengers alertly rescue themselves. "You mean the plane won't do that?" he asks. "Listen," one of them says. "This plane floats about as well as a boat flies."

Q: Why does the Pope kiss the ground each time that he lands?
A: Did you ever fly Alitalia?

"Our headline ran, *Virgin screws British Airways*. We'd have rather preferred *British Airways screws Virgin*, but we had to run with the facts."

— News Editor, *The Sun* newspaper

The Air Canada Employee Flying Club was extremely proud the day the four-seated Cessna 172, newly painted in the airline's colors, was rolled out of the hangar for the first time. It was tiny in comparison to other planes at the Toronto Maintenance Base. Flying it made for some interesting radio exchanges.

"Toronto Ground, this is Allegheny 357. I'd like taxi clearance."

Ground Control: "Roger, Allegheny. Hold short. You have an Air Canada L-1011, an Air Canada DC-8, and an Air Canada Cessna 172 passing in front."

Allegheny: "Well, I'll be. A papa bear, mama bear, and an iddy biddy baby bear."

United hired gentlemen with the expectation of training them to become pilots; Northwest hired pilots hoping to train them to become gentlemen. To date, despite their best efforts, neither carrier can be considered successful.

— Ed Thompson

"This is Captain Sinclair speaking. On behalf of my crew, I'd like to welcome you aboard British Airways Flight 602 from New York to London. We're currently flying at a height of 35,000 feet midway across the Atlantic.

If you look out of the windows on the starboard side of the aircraft, you'll observe that both the starboard engines are on fire.

If you look out of the windows on the port side, you'll observe that the port wing has fallen off.

If you look down toward the Atlantic Ocean, you'll see a little yellow life raft with three people in it waving at you.

That's me, your Captain, the co-pilot and one of the flight attendants. This is a recorded message. Have a good flight!"

Heard this one on a holiday-season Alaska Airlines flight as we were starting the descent:

"Ladies and gentlemen, this is your Captain speaking. On behalf of all of us at Alaska Airlines we'd like to thank you for flying with us today. We're beginning our descent into Los Angeles, and we'd like to ask you to stow baggage and bring your tables and seatbacks into the upright position."

"Oh, and folks, I've been reminded to inform you that, as you deplane and walk to the baggage claim area, you may notice tons and tons of mistletoe hanging at the gates of our competitors. Don't be alarmed. It's just there to remind you that, when you fly our competitors, you can just plan on kissing your luggage goodbye."

— Evan Julber, ejulber@bendnet.com

If airplanes were automobiles, most of the Northwest fleet would have historic vehicle license plates.

"Good morning, ladies and gentlemen. This is your Captain Abdo Abou Mazag welcoming you to Yemen Airlines.

We apologize for the four-day delay in taking off. It was due to bad weather and some overtime I had to put in at the bakery. This is Flight 126 to Tunis.

Landing in Tunis is not guaranteed, but we'll end up somewhere in the West. And if luck is in our favor, we may even be landing on your village. Yemen Airlines has an excellent record for safety. It's with pleasure I announce that starting this year, over 50% of our passengers have reached their destination.

To make your free fall to earth pleasant and memorable, we serve complimentary tea and biscuits!

For our not-so-religious passengers, we're the only airline that can help you find out if there really is a God!

We regret to inform you that today's in-flight movie will not be shown as we forgot to record it from the television. But for our movie buffs, we'll be flying right next to Tunis Air, where their movie will be visible from the right side of the cabin window.

There's no smoking in this airplane. Any smoke you see in the cabin is only the early warning system on the engines telling us to slow down.

To catch important landmarks, we try to fly as close as possible for the best view. If, however, we go a little too close, do let us know. Our enthusiastic co-pilot sometimes flies right through the landmark.

Kindly be seated. Keep your seat in an upright position for take-off and fasten your seat belt. For those of you who can't find a seat belt, kindly fasten your own belt to the arm of your seat. And for those who can't find a seat, don't hesitate to get in touch with a flight attendant who will explain how to fasten yourself to your suitcase."

AIRLINE ACRONYMS

Aeroflot — Areosplat
Aero Mexico — Aero Maybe
Airbus — Scarebus
Air France — Air Chance
Air New York — Air New Jerk

Allegany Airlines — Agony Air
American Airlines — Always Awful
American West — American Worst
Aspen Airways — Crashpen Airways
ATA — Alcoholics Transporting Alcoholics
British Air — Bloody Awful
BOAC — Bloody, Old and Careless
Cathay Pacific — Crash in Pacific
China Airlines — China Scarelines or Choose Another
Cubana — Castro Usually Boards Another Aircraft
DELTA — Directs Everyone's Luggage to Atlanta
DHL — Duey, Huey and Louie
Eastern (EAL) — Eastern's Always Late
Egypt Air — Gypped Air
El Al — Every Landing, Always Late
Finnair — Finished Airlines
Gulf Air — Gulp Air
Iraqi Airways — I Wrecked it Airlines
JAL — Just Arrives Late
KLM — Keeps Losing Money
Korean Air Lines — Careenin' Air Lines
Kuwait Airways — You Wait Airways
LOT — Look Out Tower
Mexicana — Wrecksicana
Midway Airlines — May Day Airlines
Northwest Airlines — Northworst Airlines
Pakistan International Airlines — Perhaps I Arrive
Pan Am Airlines — Pandemonium Airlines
PSA — People Scattered Allover
People Express — Cattle Express
SAS — Slow and Safe
Southwest — Southworst

TAP (Portuguese Air) — Take Another Plane
Texas Air — Wrecks Us Air
TWA — Teeny Weenie Airlines
USAir — Useless Air or You Still Allegany
United — Ur Never Intended to Ever Depart
ValuJet — Junk Jet
Yugoslav Airlines (JAT) — Joke About Time

NO-FRILLS AIRLINE

They don't sell tickets. They sell chances.

All the insurance machines in the terminal are sold out.

Before the flight, the passengers get together and elect a pilot.

You can't board the plane unless you have the exact change.

Before you take off, the flight attendant tells you to fasten your Velcro.

The Captain asks all the passengers to chip in a little for gas.

When they pull the steps away, the plane starts rocking.

The Captain yells at the ground crew to get the cows off the runway.

You ask the Captain how often their planes crash and he says, "Just once."

No movie. Don't need one. Your life keeps flashing before your eyes.

You see a man with a gun, but he's demanding to be let off the plane.

All the planes have both a bathroom and a chapel.

Northwest is working with Boeing to develop an aircraft specific to their needs. Their first one will be the 7 & 7.

USAir recently introduced a special half-fare for wives who accompanied their husbands on business trips. Expecting valuable testimonials, the PR department sent out letters to all the wives of businessmen who had used the special rates, asking how they enjoyed their trip. Letters are still pouring in asking, "What trip?"

No one was quite sure how Pan-Am could lose an engine from an airplane. But it was found later. That was because the engine had a luggage sticker on it.

Southwest Airlines makes humor their first priority. The president of Southwest says that if you don't have a sense of humor, you'll never be hired at Southwest. If you've ever flown Southwest, you'll hear a few of these lines and many others. A frequent line used at the end of a flight is, "Our flight attendants are now walking through the aisles with trash receptacles for any garbage you might have or anything else that you might wanna give us!"

In the early sixties, Alaska Airlines was referred to as "spastic airlines" by Alaskans, and not without some cause.
Location: Anchorage International. Time: Early morning.
"Anchorage ground. Time check please." (pregnant pause)
"What airline are you?" (a longer pregnant pause)
"Ah, er, uuum, does it make a difference?"
Whereupon a bright and effervescent voice says, "Oh, yes! If you're Pan Am, it's zero eight hundred. If you're Wein, it's eight AM.
"But if you're Alaska Airlines, the little hand is on eight and the big hand is on twelve!"
— Larry, denali@ilhawaii.net

AIRLINE SECURITY - AIR MARSHALL INSTRUCTIONS

PA plays *Onward Christian Soldiers* while boarding. Gate agents and flight attendants look for distressed reactions. (Oui Vey sighs may be disregarded)

Insert copies of Salmon Rushdie's *The Satanic Verses* in seat-backs along with emergency information. Flight attendants look for adverse reactions during pushback.

Engage suspicious persons in polite conversation. Ask if the Taliban has a dental plan.

Install *Beware of Dog* sign in Arabic on cockpit door.

Install *Flight Deck* sign in Arabic on forward lavatory.

After takeoff, initiate a series of 360-degree turns. Would-be terrorists become dizzy or strain necks trying to face Mecca.

Install impaling spikes outside the cockpit door that will activate on impact or by triggering.

First Officers only are required to carry guns. This avoids either pilot being killed in crossfire.

Peephole in door replaced with porthole through which a flight attendant sticks head prior to entry. Should head of persona-non-grata poke through, the guillotine would fall, head would drop through chute and roll back into cabin through the trap door as message for potential "sleepers."

Live video of subdued hijackers being garroted in first class shown in lieu of movie. Complimentary headsets provided.

The temperature at our destination is fifty degrees with some broken clouds, but we'll try to have them fixed before we arrive. Thank you and remember, nobody loves you or your money, more than Southwest Airlines.

Near the conclusion of an extremely turbulent American Airlines flight, a cabin attendant finished his "stowed-tray-table-and-upright-seat" speech with a cheerful, "We'd like to thank you for flying American Airlines. But if you were displeased with the flight, thank you for flying United."

"Good evening, ladies and gentlemen, this is your Captain speaking. Thank you for flying Vapor Air 324 nonstop from London to New York. We're still awaiting our security clearance from U.S. authorities, but it's safe to assume that we'll land in New York sometime next month or so.

If you look to your left, you'll see a landmark that attracts more than one million tourists every year. It's called Heathrow Airport. Yes, we haven't yet taken off as a few astute passengers have noticed. Needless to say, we'd rather wait on the ground than in the air. It's so much easier to get a refill. You won't believe how fast we go through our liquor cart.

The weather in New York is cold and breezy, with a thirty percent chance of snow. But why am I telling you that? By the time we get there, it might be summer.

Of course, there's still a possibility the status of this flight will be changed to delayed indefinitely from its current status of delayed definitely. If that happens, you may be asked to disembark immediately. With that in mind, I advise you not to get too comfortable. You may recline your seat and stretch your legs, but please don't change into your pajamas.

If you're spotted wearing pajamas in the airport, the United States may revoke your visa. In fact, if you're seen wearing any type of clothing that does not conform to standards established by the U.S. Attorney General, as specified in Section IV, Paragraph 3 of the Anti-Terrorism Law, you may be denied entry into the United States, unless, of course, you can prove you're a member of the clergy. Please don't take this personally. These measures have been taken to protect you from people who look like you.

As you've probably heard, the U.S. government recently raised the national threat level to orange, which means there's a high risk of terrorists attacking people with oranges. This may seem like a minor threat to you, but has anyone ever squeezed an orange into your eye?

As a result of this threat, airport security has been beefed up, with apologies to our vegetarian passengers. Some of you already know this, having spent the last two hours being poked at. A few of you may have come under extra scrutiny, especially if you have names such as Hussein, Ahmed, and Abdul. But most of you are white and your names, thankfully, create no concern, as I just told the three men in first class, an Englishman named Hunt, an American named Rob, and a Dutchman named Harm.

Once we get to New York, you may be photographed and fingerprinted, especially if you come from a non-European country. Please don't take this personally. No one is saying that you're a terrorist. They're just saying that you look like one.

Before I finish, I'd like to draw your attention to the back of the plane, where you'll see that we have an Indian man flying with us today. Please don't panic. He's been through a special sixteen hour security check. We even tested the oil in his hair. You'll be glad to know that it isn't flammable. Among the items we've confiscated from this man are two sharp pencils, one orange, and a bottle of a caustic, tongue-burning substance that he claims is lemon pickle.

Anyway, I just want you to know that this man will soon get up to use the restroom, escorted by three armed flight marshals.

His activities in the restroom will be observed with 206 cameras, one for every bone in his body. He's been instructed to keep his hands raised above his head at all times, so you might not want to use the restroom after him.

Why am I telling you all of this? Well, I'm retiring in a couple of months, and I feel a strong urge to be completely open with my passengers, an urge I've had ever since the liquor cart went by."

Thank you for flying Delta Business Express. We hope you enjoyed giving us the business as much as we enjoyed taking you for a ride.

And from the pilot during his welcome message: "Delta Airlines is pleased to have some of the best flight attendants in the industry. Unfortunately, none of them are on this flight."

Heard on a pre-flight announcement from an American Airlines pilot:

"On our flight today, we'll be flying at 34,000 feet. To give you an idea of how high that is, we'd be able to fly over fifty Empire State buildings stacked one on top the other. Our speed will be about 500 miles per hour. That is just over the muzzle velocity of the standard military .45 pistol. We'll be pushed along by two Pratt and Whitney JT-8D-200 turbofan engines. While thrust to horsepower varies with altitude, the total 40,000 pounds of thrust is greater than the combined power of ten D-9 diesel locomotives.

In other words, we're faster than a speeding bullet, more powerful than a locomotive, and able to leap tall buildings in a single bound, and as always, your Dallas based crew stands for truth, justice, and the *American* way!"

While taxiing out behind a Lufthansa airliner at Frankfurt, a C-130 (Hercules) crew noticed an orange *Remove Before Flight* streamer hanging out of the Lufthansa nose wheel well (their nose gear locking pin was still installed). Not wanting to cause too much embarrassment by going through the controller, the C-130 crew simply called the Lufthansa aircraft on the tower frequency: "Lufthansa aircraft, Herky 23." No reply.

They repeated the transmission, and again there was no reply. Instead, the Lufthansa pilot called the tower and asked the tower to tell the Herky crew that "the professional pilots of Lufthansa do not engage in unprofessional conversations over the radio."

The 130 pilot quickly replied, "Frankfurt tower, can you please relay to the professional pilots of the Lufthansa aircraft that their nose gear pin is still installed?"

At the airport for a family trip, I settled down to wait for the boarding announcement at Gate 35. Then I heard the voice on the public address system saying, "We apologize for the inconvenience, but Delta flight 570 will board from gate 41."

So my family picked up our luggage and carried it over to gate 41. Not ten minutes later the public address voice told us that flight 570 would, in fact, be boarding from gate 35.

So, again, we gathered our carry-on luggage and returned to the original gate. Just as we were settling down, the public address voice spoke again: "Thank you for participating in Delta's physical fitness program."

HELP FEED DELTA PILOTS

It's just not right. Thousands of pilots in our very own country are living at or just below the six figure salary line.

And if that wasn't bad enough, many may go several weeks or months without a paycheck if they're forced by Delta Airlines management to strike.

But now you can help. For about three hundred dollars a day (that's less than the price of a 25" television set) you can help keep a pilot economically viable during his/her time of need. Three hundred dollars a day may not seem like a lot of money to you, but to a pilot, it could mean the difference between a vacation fishing in Florida or a Mediterranean cruise.

For you, three hundred dollars is nothing more than half a month's rent or mortgage payment. But to a pilot, three hundred dollars a day will almost replace his or her salary.

Three hundred dollars a day will enable a pilot to upgrade his or her home computer, buy that new 100" television set, trade in the six month old Lexus for a Ferrari, or enjoy a dinner (with champagne) at The Mansion.

HOW WILL I KNOW I'M HELPING?

Each month, you'll receive a complete financial report on the crew member you sponsor. Detailed information about his or her stocks, bonds, 401K, and real-estate holdings will be mailed to your home. You'll be able to watch your pilot's net worth grow. You'll also get information on how he/she chooses to invest the 1.2 million dollar lump sum the pilot will get upon his/her retirement.

HOW WILL THEY KNOW I'M HELPING?

Your pilot will be told that he or she has a Special Friend who just wants to help. Although the pilot won't know your name, he or she will be able to make collect calls to your home via a special operator in case the pilot needs more funds.

I want to help! In the event of a strike by the Delta pilots, I'd like to sponsor the crew member listed below (circle your selection(s):

___CAPTAIN   ___F-100 CREW MEMBER

___AN ENTIRE FLIGHT   ___A300 CREW MEMBER
   CREW

___FIRST OFFICER   ___SUPER-80 CREW MEMBER

___NAVIGATOR   ___727 CREW MEMBER

___767 CREW MEMBER   ___MD-11 CREW MEMBER

___Please apply my donation to the crew member most in need.

___Please charge the account listed below $326.25 per day (or $350.29 for MD-11 crew members) for the duration of the strike.

Please send me a picture of the crew member I've sponsored, along with a set of "wings" (while supplies last).

Mastercard [ ] Visa [ ] American Express [ ]

Diner's Club [ ] Delta Card [ ] Discover Card [ ]

Account Number: _____

Exp. Date: _____

Signature: _____

Send Completed Forms to the Delta Pilots Assoc.

Or, Enroll By Phone: (XXX)-988-3188

Note: Sponsors agree not to contact the crew member sponsored or his/her families in person or by other means including, but not limited to, phone calls, letters, email, or third parties. Contributions made are not tax deductible. In the event of no strike action taken, sponsors agree to a one-time charge of $500.00 to cover administration costs of this program.

AIRLINES AS OPERATING SYSTEMS

Air DOS: Everybody pushes the airplane until it glides, then they jump on and let the plane coast until it hits the ground again. Then they push again, jump on again, and so on.

Windows Air: The terminal is pretty and colorful, with friendly stewards, easy baggage check and boarding, and a smooth take-off. After about ten minutes in the air, the plane explodes with no warning whatsoever.

Mac Airlines: All the stewards, captains, baggage handlers, and ticket agents look and act exactly the same. Every time you ask questions about details, you're gently but firmly told that you don't need to know, don't want to know, and everything will be done for you without your ever having to know, so just shut up.

Windows NT Air: Just like Windows Air, but costs more, uses much bigger planes, and takes out all the other aircraft within a forty mile radius when it explodes.

UNIX Airways: Everyone brings one piece of the plane along when they come to the airport. They all go out on the runway and put the plane together piece by piece, arguing non-stop about what kind of plane they're supposed to be building.

Linux Air: Disgruntled employees of all the other OS airlines decide to start their own airline. They build the planes, ticket counters, and pave the runways themselves. They charge a small fee to cover the cost of printing the ticket, but you can also download and print the ticket yourself. When you board the plane, you're given a seat, four bolts, a wrench, and a copy of the seat-HOWTO.html. Once settled, the fully adjustable seat is comfortable; the plane leaves, and arrives on time without a single problem. The in-flight meal is wonderful. You try to tell customers of the other airlines about the great trip, but all they can say is, "You had to do *what* with the seat?"

DOS with QEMM: Same as DOS, but with more leg room for pushing.

OS/2: To get on board, you must have your ticket stamped ten different times by standing in ten different lines. Then you fill out a form asking how you want your seating arranged. With the look and feel of an ocean liner, a passenger train, or a bus. If you get on board and off the ground, you'll have a wonderful trip, except when the rudder and flaps freeze, in which case you have time to say your prayers before you crash.

NT: The terminal and flight attendants all look like those the Windows plane uses, but the process of checking in and going through security is a nightmare. Once aboard, those passengers with first class tickets can go anywhere they want and arrive in half the time, while the vast majority of passengers with coach tickets can't even get aboard.

CAIRO: The airplane is distributed among 47 different hangars in thirteen airports scattered over eight states, four Canadian provinces, and a remote mountain hideaway in Nicaragua. But you don't need to know where the airplane is or who it belongs to in order to fly it. Actually, you don't fly the airplane itself; you fly a simulation that behaves just like the real thing except that you don't go anywhere. But that's okay, because when the world is at your fingertips. You never need to leave home.

NINE

Aircraft

Comment in the New York Times editorial page of December 10, 1903, just one week before the successful flight at Kitty Hawk by the Wright brothers:

"We hope that Professor Langley will not put his substantial greatness as a scientist in further peril by continuing to waste his time and the money involved in further airship experiments. Life is short, and he is capable of services to humanity incomparably greater than can be expected to result from trying to fly. For students and investigators of the Langley type, there are more useful employments."

"Orville! Call the bike shop. We're in deep trouble. Ma wants her bed sheets back!"

— Wilbur Wright

It's said that two wrongs do not make a right, but two Wrights do make an aeroplane.

"No flying machine will ever fly from New York to Paris."

— Orville Wright

"The Wright Brothers created the single greatest cultural force since the invention of writing. The airplane became the first World Wide Web, bringing people, languages, ideas, and values together."

— Bill Gates, CEO, Microsoft Corporation

"Both optimists and pessimists contribute to the society. The optimist invents the aeroplane; the pessimist, the parachute."

— George Bernard Shaw

I read today that the Boeing 777 has five million lines of computer code. Bet you won't see too many programmers flying in those babies!

Pilots flying heavy iron[2] are sometimes known for their lighthearted jibes at pilots of smaller aircraft.

One day at Toronto's Pearson International Airport, an A-340 was in line for departure behind a Fokker[3] F-28, an aircraft that has a tail that splits to act as a large speed brake[4]. The Airbus captain was heard on the radio, making some comment about the "cute little plane" in front of him and boasting about the brand new jumbo he was flying.

In response, the Fokker's fuselage speed brakes opened wide, and over the radio an explosive, "Pbbbbbbbt!" was heard.

"I do believe we've been the target of a fart!" said the A-340 first officer to his Captain.

---

2 777s, 747s, Airbus, etc. Da big 'uns.
3 Nickname for Focke-Wulf aircraft
4 Enables unusually fast deceleration by disturbing the air flow.

"And this, ladies and gentlemen, is the very first Fokker airplane built in the world. The Dutch call it the mother Fokker."
— Custodian at the Aviodome aviation museum,
Schiphol airport, Amsterdam

"Heard in a Lufthansa Boeing 747-400 cockpit: Have you heard about the bird strike of the Airbus 340? It happened over the North Atlantic. It was hit by a bird. From behind!"
— Guido Frey

"Lady, you want me to answer you if this old airplane is safe to fly? Just how in the world do you think it got to be this old?"
— Jim Tavenner

"Airplanes may kill you, but they ain't likely to hurt you."
— 'Satchel' (Leroy Robert)
Paige, baseball player

"If black boxes survive air crashes, why don't they make the whole plane out of that stuff?"
— George Carlin

If it ain't broke, don't fix it. If it ain't fixed, don't fly it.

Fuel in the tanks is limited. Gravity is forever.
Never trust a fuel gauge.
Aviate, Navigate, Communicate.
Keep the shiny side up and greasy side down

What's the difference between an Airbus A-320 and a Black & Decker chain saw? About 320 trees a minute.

Remember folks, if it ain't Boeing, I ain't going!

"The Piper Cub is the safest airplane in the world; it can just barely kill you."
　　　　　　　　　　　— Max Stanley, Northrop test pilot

A commuter flight in Australia is holding for a 747 on takeoff in bad weather. The 747 starts the takeoff roll but aborts just before the point of no return. The incident report said that the aircraft had aborted because it had lost power in one engine.

The 747 was full of people taking their first flight after a course to overcome the fear of flying.

Apparently, an owner of an Aztec in Africa had an engine problem in some rather remote location and was considering trying to take off and fly the airplane on one engine to a maintenance base. The message he sent to Piper's engineering department ended with the question, "How long will it take to take off on one engine?"

This request for information made its rounds within engineering until it got to the Aztec project engineer who replied, "Ask him if he wants that in miles or months."

The owner's guide that comes with a $500 refrigerator makes more sense than the one that comes with a $50 million airliner.

If it's ugly, it's British. If it's weird, it's French. And if it's ugly and weird, it's Russian.

An RV-6 owner attended a breakfast fly-in and put the airplane on the static display line. A three-year-old hopped up on the wing, pointed to the yoke-mounted Lowrance AirMap 300 handheld GPS, and said: "Look, Ma, he's got a Gameboy!"

French aviation authorities here admitted to a near-disaster which occurred aboard an Airbus A320 jetliner. The controversial aircraft with its "fly-by-wire" flight controls has been the subject of intense controversy since its introduction.

The manufacturer, a consortium of European interests, has steadfastly maintained the aircraft's inherent safety over other aircraft, largely as a result of the computerized controls that limit inputs from the pilots to ensure they're always compatible with the current aerodynamic state of the plane.

Pilots and pundits have argued that these same safeguards can severely limit the crew's options in emergency conditions. Additionally, they argue that the increased faith placed in the on-board computers leads to crew complacency and inattentiveness.

The incident in question took place while the aircraft, a British Airways plane, was at cruise altitude between New York and Fairbanks. The co-pilot was apparently entering new navigational data into the craft's INS (Inertial Navigation System) when he miss-typed a code. The INS came back with "Invalid PIN number selected" and returned the craft's weight and balance data to the astonished crew.

"We tried several more times," exclaimed Reginald Dwight, the Captain, "and every time it was the same thing. On the third try it said *Access violation, contact your credit institution if you believe there is an error.* At that point all the plane's controls froze, and it refused to respond to our commands. We didn't know what to do, so we got on the radio."

British Airways' mechanics were equally dumbfounded and decided to call French mechanics. France's Aerospatial is the prime contractor for the aircraft. "The French were totally rude to us," stated an unnamed BA mechanic. "They stated the problem was our fault and that 'the pasty little Englishman probably had too many meat pies and Guinness.' It wasn't until we told them that Jerry Lewis was aboard the flight that they became concerned."

French mechanics traced the problem to the ATM-6000 INS computer, which was a modified version of a computer used in the United States for bank transactions. Essentially, the INS decided that the co-pilot was trying to rip-off someone and locked the controls. French authorities then assured the English crew that the system would automatically remove the restrictions at the start of the next banking day. "We told them that we would be in the sea by then!" exclaimed the frustrated co-pilot, Nigel Whitworth.

A French team, headed by Bertrand Swatboutie, determined that manual control of the plane could be re-established if a crewmember went back to the tail cone and operated the elevators manually. The rudder is linked by backup cables to the cockpit.

With the crewmember operating the elevator, they determined they would have enough control. "There's nothing wrong with ze plane," exclaimed Swatboutie, "that a little pinch in the rear will not cure. Just like a woman. If these English souffres[5] knew anything about women, they would never have had to call us in the first place."

The plane was able to safely land at Denver's Stapleton airport, where the craft was repaired and all crewmembers' credit histories were reviewed.

At a recent software engineering management course in the U.S., the participants were given an awkward question to answer.

---

5 Wimps

"If you had just boarded an airliner and discovered that your team of programmers had been responsible for the flight control software, how many of you would disembark immediately?"

Among the ensuing forest of raised hands, only one man sat motionless. When asked what he would do, he replied that he would be quite content to stay onboard. "With this team's software," he said, "the plane was unlikely to even taxi as far as the runway, let alone take off."

An airline flight attendant was giving the standard safety briefing to the passengers. She had just finished saying "In the event of a water landing, your seat cushion may be used as a flotation device," when a man remarked, "Hey! If the plane can't fly, why should I believe the seat can float?"

WHY AIRPLANES ARE BETTER THAN WOMEN:

More than two people can participate in any flight.

Airplanes don't have parents.

Airplanes don't get pregnant.

Airplanes don't get jealous if you fly another plane.

Airplanes don't insult you if you do something wrong.

Your parents don't keep in touch with a plane after you replace it.

Airplanes don't care if you're late.

Airplanes can be warmed up in five minutes.

Airplanes don't ask for protection before you board.

Airplanes depreciate less the more you use them.

You can still ride a fifty-year-old airplane.

You can predict an airplane.

If you respect an airplane, it will be good to you.

Airplane skin doesn't wrinkle as badly.

Airplanes don't comment on your piloting skills.

An airplane doesn't care where you were last night.

Airplanes don't care how many other airplanes you've flown before.

Airplanes don't cost as much money.

Airplanes don't take forever to warm up.

Airplanes like to do it inverted.

Airplanes won't keep you waiting.

Airplanes won't insist you shower before entering it.

Airplanes don't cry when you break up with them.

Airplanes don't talk back.

Airplanes don't get headaches.

Airplanes don't take half of everything.

Airplanes never stand you up.

An airplane is cheaper to maintain.

You can't get diseases from an airplane.

Airplanes don't care if you fart.

You can keep an airplane from stalling.

Airplanes can be turned on by a flick of a switch.

You can approach an airplane from the rear.

You can proudly show off your airplane inside and out.

An airplane won't slap you for being a "bush pilot."

You can easily leave an airplane before sunrise.

Airplanes lose weight faster.

You don't always have to "hand prop" an airplane.

Airplanes don't care if you fall asleep while in them.

Airplanes don't get mad if you "touch and go."

An airplane won't get mad if you ride someone else's airplane.

You can calculate the peak performance of an airplane.

An airplane is easy to roll over.

Airplanes expect to be tied down.

Airplanes don't need as much lubrication.

Airplanes don't droop after ten years.

Airplanes are easy to love.

You don't have to sweet-talk an airplane.

You can always tell when an airplane is going to give out.

An airplane moves when you tell it to.

An airplane goes anywhere you direct it to.

Wide body airplanes are still attractive.

An airplane will kill you quickly. A woman takes her time.

An airplane takes less time to turn around.

An airplane doesn't object to a preflight inspection.

Airplanes don't make you "pull-out" to eject.

Airplanes come with manuals to explain their operation.

Airplanes can handle thrust better.

Airplanes don't scream.

A 747 can keep going for up to fourteen hours.

You can adjust an airplane's attitude easily.

Airplanes have strict weight and balance limits.

Airplanes have ashtrays and tray tables.

When you put fuel into an airplane, it won't spit it out.

Sometimes you can ride airplanes for free.

It's easier to understand what an airplane needs.

You can fly an airplane any time of the month.

Airplanes don't whine unless something is really wrong.

Airplanes and pilots both arrive at the same time.

Airplanes don't mind if you look at other airplanes, or if you buy airplane magazines.

However, when airplanes go quiet, just like women, it's a bad thing.

WHY WOMEN PREFER AIRPLANES OVER MEN:

An airplane takes gas. A man passes it.

Airplanes can be turned off when you don't wish to fly.

An airplane doesn't "let down" before it's time.

With an airplane, size matters.

Airplanes can be overhauled when the engine sputters.

Airplanes don't perform over-gross.

Airplanes don't come with drinking buddies.

Airplanes eventually stop whining.

Airplanes use drag, thrust, weight and balance as a checklist.

Airplanes know what a final approach is.

Airplanes don't mind if you "position and hold."

In an airplane, a soft field landing isn't a disappointment.

Airplanes don't mind if you'd rather just cuddle.

Only toy airplanes run by remote control.

SANTA CLAUS AIRCRAFT SPECIFICATIONS

The Santa Sleigh is a versatile, all-weather, multi-purpose, vertical short-take-off and landing vehicle. It's capable of travelling vast distances without refueling. The sleigh can be deployed anywhere in the world to support Santa's goodwill mission, but only on Christmas Eve.

The Santa Sleigh has been equipped with the latest navigational aids including GPS. One of its most notable features is its ability to deliver a vast array of presents with pinpoint accuracy.

Designer & Builder: K. Kringle & Elves Inc.

First flight: December 24, 343 A.D.

Localization of Sleigh: North Pole

Length: 75 cc (candy canes)/150 lp (lollipops).

Width: 40 cc/80 lp.

Height: 55 cc/110 lp.

Sleigh weight at take-off: 75,000 gd (gumdrops).

Passenger weight at take-off: Santa Claus, 260 pounds.

Miscellaneous weight at take-off: 60,000 tons of presents.

Sleigh weight at landing: 80,000 gd (ice & snow accumulation).

Passenger weight at landing: 260 pounds + 60,000 tons of cookies.

Propulsion: 9 rp (reindeer power).

Armament: Antlers (purely defensive).

Fuel: Reindeer consume low octane organic fuels (hay)

Emissions: Classified.

Climbing speed: In the twinkle of an eye.

Maximum speed: Faster than starlight.

Note: Length, width, and height are determined without reindeer.

TEN

Aircraft Maintenance

YOU MIGHT BE AN AIRCRAFT MECHANIC IF:

You've ever slept on the concrete under a wing.

You've ever said, "Oh, yes, sir, it's supposed to look like that."

You know what JP-4[6] or 145 octane tastes like.

You have a better bench-stock in the pockets of your coveralls than in the shop.

You've ever used a piece of safety wire as a toothpick.

You've ever worked a 14-hour shift on an aircraft that isn't flying the next day.

You can sleep anywhere, anytime, but as soon as the engines shut down you're wide awake.

You've ever stood on wheel chock[7]s to keep your feet dry.

Wondered where they keep finding the idiots who keep making up stupid rules.

You've ever had to defuel an aircraft an hour after refueling it.

You know more about your co-workers than your own family.

---

6 Jet fuel
7 Wedge to stop wheel from turning

You've ever wished the pilot would say "Great Airplane."

You've ever wondered why it takes a college degree to break an airplane, but only a high school diploma to fix one.

You've ever used a wooden chock as a pillow while sleeping on a pushback tug.

You've ever scuba dived a lavatory tank to remove everything under the sun.

You've ever screwed up something really expensive.

You've told someone that you're an aircraft mechanic only to have him or her say, "But not on the engines.... Right?"

You've wanted to put your foot up a pilot's butt on many occasions.

You've ever wished that you had chosen a different career.

— Bob Oberst

TROUBLE TICKETS

Problem: Something loose in cockpit.

Solution: Something tightened in cockpit.

Problem: The autopilot doesn't.

Solution: It Does Now.

Problem: Number three engine missing.

Solution: Engine found on right wing after brief search.

Problem: Noise coming from #1 engine. Sounds like little man with a hammer.

Solution: Took hammer away from little man.

Problem: Whining noise coming from #1 engine.

Solution: Returned hammer to little man.

Problem: Flight attendant cold at altitude.

Solution: Ground checks okay.

Problem: Target Radar hums.

Solution: Reprogrammed Target Radar with the lyrics.

Problem: Evidence of hydraulic leak on right main landing gear.

Solution: Evidence removed.

Problem: DME[8] volume unbelievably loud.

Solution: Volume set to more believable level.

Problem: Autopilot tends to drop a wing when fuel imbalance reaches 500 lbs.

Solution: Flight manual limits maximum fuel imbalance to 300 lbs.

Problem: Aircraft climbs like its tired.

Solution: Aircraft rested overnight. Ground checks okay.

Problem: Flight attendants complain of numerous roaches in the galleys.

Solution: Roaches deplaned.

Problem: Dead bugs on windshield.

Solution: Live bugs on order.

Problem: IFF[9] inoperative.

Solution: IFF always inoperative in OFF mode.

Problem: Friction locks cause throttle levers to stick.

Solution: That's what they're there for!

Problem: Aircraft handles funny.

Solution: Aircraft warned to "Straighten up, fly right, and be serious."

Problem: Test flight OK, except Autoland rough.

Solution: Autoland not installed on this aircraft.

Problem: No. 2 propeller seeping prop fluid.

Solution: No. 2 propeller seepage normal. Numbers 1, 3, and 4 propellers lack normal seepage.

Problem: Suspected crack in windscreen.

Solution: Suspect you're right.

---

8 Distance Measuring Equipment
9 Identification Friend or Foe

Problem: Mouse in cockpit.

Solution: Cat installed.

Problem: Autopilot in "altitude-hold" mode produces a 200-fpm descent.

Solution: Cannot reproduce problem on ground.

Problem: Radio switches stick.

Solution: Peanut butter no longer served to flight crew.

Problem: Screaming sound in cabin at start-up.

Solution: Company accountant deplaned.

Problem: Funny smell in cockpit.

Solution: Pilot told to change cologne.

Problem: #3 engine knocks at idle.

Solution: #3 engine let in for a few beers.

Problem: #3 engine runs like its sick.

Solution: #3 engine diagnosed with hangover.

Problem: Brakes howl on application.

Solution: Don't step on 'em so hard!

Problem: Radio sounds like a squealing pig.

Solution: Removed pig from radio. BBQ behind hangar tomorrow.

Problem: Whole aircraft smells like BBQ.

Solution: Ground checks okay.

Problem: First class cabin floor has a squeak.

Solution: Co-pilot told not to play with toddler toys in cabin anymore.

Problem: Electrical governor is broke.

Solution: Paid off governor's debt to Jimmy "The Fish" Galvano.

Midnight shift mechanics don't enjoy last minute radio calls from flight crews as the sun comes up. If there's a problem, let us know before it's time to push back.

Early one morning, a UAL co-pilot had some minor complaint with his flying machine.

"Portland maintenance, United 2246."

I was closest to the radio and intoned in a grave voice: "What is the nature of your sin, my son?"

"Uhhh, disregard."

— Buzz Fuseasausage, meyer5pdx@juno.com

Many years ago, in my time as a Customs Officer at Melbourne Airport (Australia, not Florida), a JAT (Yugoslavian Airlines) pilot was inspecting his plane with the ground engineer before take-off. Normally, this means just making sure that the wings and engines were in the right places in the right amounts.

This day, however, the ground engineer noticed that there was a fuel leak from a wing tank. He brought this to the notice of the pilot who nonchalantly dismissed the problem with the comment, "No worries. We get to 30,000 feet, she freeze up. No problem." (Told to me by the ground engineer)

— eorenstein@swin.edu.au (Earle Orenstein)

A couple of drinkin' buddies, who are airplane mechanics, are in the hanger at SFO[10]. It's fogged in, and they have nothing to do.

One of them says to the other, "Man, have you got anything to drink?"

"Nah, but I hear you can drink jet fuel. That'll kinda give you a buzz." So they do, get smashed, and have a beautiful time like only drinkin' buddies can do.

The following morning, one of them wakes up and knows his head will explode if he gets up. But it doesn't. He gets up and feels good. In fact, he feels great! *No hangover!*

---

10 San Francisco airport

The phone rings; it's his buddy. The buddy says, "Hey, how do you feel?"

He said, "I feel great!"

The buddy says, "I feel great too! You don't have a hangover?"

He says "No. That jet fuel is great stuff. No hangover. We ought to do this more often."

"Yeah, we could, but there's just one thing."

"What's that?"

"Did you fart yet?"

"What?"

"Did you *fart* yet?"

"No."

"Well, *don't*, 'cause I'm in Phoenix!"

— Jos van Wunnik, trinitys@airmail.net

Two airline mechanics were working on a 747 when lunch-time came. Rather than leave what they were doing, they just took their lunch break while sitting in the cockpit. While they were eating lunch, one mechanic bet the other that the landing gear wouldn't retract if he pulled the gear lever up.

He lost.

I fixed it right the first time. It must have failed for other reasons.

Your plane will be ready by two o'clock.

ELEVEN

Lingo Decoded

FLIGHT CREW CODE WORDS:

Choppy Air — severe turbulence

Hockey Puck — tasteless deli sandwich

Jetbag — very senior flight attendant

New Arrival Time — late!

NFR — 'Nother Friggin' Runner (passenger arriving late)

Restricted Visibility — a white-out or bad fog

Self-loading cargo — passengers

Showers — severe thunderstorm

Slam Dunk — very hard landing

Slider — tasteless breakfast omelet

PASSENGER GLOSSARY

Air Traffic Control: A game played by airline pilots and air traffic controllers. The game has no rules, and neither side knows how it's played, but the goal is to prevent flights from arriving in time for passengers to make connecting flights.

Airline Meals: A reminder that you should have eaten before you left. The little bags in the seat backs are for those who wish to try the food.

Baggage Claim: The most far away and difficult area of the airport to find. It's usually hidden by numerous signs saying, *Baggage Claim Area.*

Departure Gate: This is where the most uncomfortable seats are tested by many young and tired children.

First Class: Where the people sit who didn't throw away all their money on fast food and beer.

Flight Schedule: Fictitious reading material to occupy and entertain a traveler's waiting time.

Fog: A natural weather phenomenon, which usually occurs around an airport while the surrounding areas are clear. Fog is controlled by the airlines and used to delay flights.

Group: A large, loud pack of passengers travelling together. The group leader, who has the tickets, usually waits in the bar spending all the emergency stipend until the required pre-board time of five minutes before departure, or until there are no seats left together, whichever occurs last. Reservation agents are prohibited from pre-assigning seats to groups as this may convenience them.

Next Flight: Perhaps tomorrow afternoon.

No-Record: Any passenger booked through a travel agency.

Non-Revenue Position: Usually can be identified by the fact that these passengers are in first class and are dressed in pilot or flight attendant uniforms. Non-revenue positions are permitted to fly first class free of charge to prevent revenue passengers from being able to upgrade to first class.

Occupied: An airline term for lavatory.

On Time: An obscure term with unknown meaning.

Passenger: A herding creature of widely varying intellect, usually found in pairs or small groups. Often will become vicious and violent in simple and easily rectified situations.

When frightened or confused, these creatures collect into a group called a "line." This "line" has no set pattern and is usually formed in inconvenient places. Passengers are of four known species: Paxus iratus, Paxus latus, Paxus inebriatus, and Paxus ignoramus.

Position Closed: This is a sign posted at various counter locations, interpreted by the passenger to mean: "Form Line Here."

Pre-Board: Passenger who arrives at the gate five minutes before departure.

Restrooms: The tiny cubicle that attracts the fat lady with constipation. The remaining cubicle contains the crew's extra luggage.

Schedule: This is where you rush to leave your home airport at 5:30 am to arrive at the nearby hub airport where you have a four-hour layover.

Sign: An airport decoration. Usually unnoticed except by small children. Its primary function is to hide the location of various areas of the airport, i.e., gate numbers, restrooms, baggage claim, etc.

Ticket: The voucher you'll need to rebook with another airline after your flight was canceled.

Ticket Agent: A superhuman with the patience of a saint, the herding ability of an Australian sheepdog, the E.S.P. abilities of Uri Geller, the compassion of a psychoanalyst and the tact of a diplomat. They have mysterious abilities to control wind/rain/snow/fog and all other weather phenomenon. They're capable of answering three questions at a time while talking on the phone, without stuttering or choking on their tongues. In later life, they carry on mysterious conversations with themselves.

PILOT GLOSSARY

180-Degree Turn: A sometimes difficult maneuver to perform; the degree of difficulty usually determined by the size of the pilot's ego.

A & P Rating: Enables you to fly grocery supplies. [11]

Aero: That portion of the atmosphere that lies over Great Britain.

Aerodrome: British word for airport. Exactly what you'd expect from a country that gives its airplanes names like Gypsy Moth, Slingsby Dart, and Fairey Battle Bomber.

Aileron: A hinged control surface on the rear of the wing that scares the hell out of airline passengers when it moves.

Airplane: The infernal machine invented by two bicycle mechanics from Dayton, OH and perfected on the sands of the Outer Banks of Kitty Hawk, NC. Precursor of the Frisbee.

Airspeed:
- The speed of an airplane through the air.
- Deduct 25% when listening to a Navy aviator.
- Measured in furlongs-per-fortnight in student aircraft.

Airstrip: In-flight performance by exotic female flight attendant.

Air Traffic Control Center: A drafty, ill-kept, barn-like structure in which people congregate for dubious reasons.

Air Traffic Controller: A federal employee, usually a retired tobacco auctioneer, assigned to a major airport to keep aircraft from landing in unison. This is accomplished by giving rapid instructions over the radio, most of which mean to go away and come back again, preferably after the air traffic controller is off duty.

Alternate Airport:
- The airport that no aircraft has sufficient fuel to proceed to if necessary.

---

11 Airframe and power plant qualified

- The area directly beyond the active runway when the engine quits on take-off. [12]

Altimeter Setting: The place where the altimeter sets. Usually hidden by the control column during a near-minimums instrument approach. [13]

Angle of Attack: Pick-up lines that pilots use. [14]

Arctic Frost: Attitude shown by uncooperative stewardess (also see "Horizontally Opposed").

Arresting Gear: Police equipment used for keeping order at airport parties. [15]

Bail Out: Dipping the water out of the cabin after a heavy rainstorm.

Bank: The folks who hold the mortgage on your aircraft and Corvette. [16]

Barrel Roll: Unloading the beer for a hangar party. [17]

Captain:

- Any airline pilot wearing four stripes on his sleeve. Often found strolling down Lover's Lane holding his own hand.
- Decorative dummy often found adorning the bridge of a ship.

Carburetor Icing: A phenomenon that happens to pilots at exactly the same time they run out of gas.

Certificated Aircraft: One that has all hazardous features camouflaged.

Chart:

- Large piece of paper, useful for protecting cockpit surfaces from food and beverage stains.

---

12 Different airport for emergencies
13 Measures altitude
14 Angle the wing hits the airstream
15 Cable to stop aircraft very quickly
16 Turn made in flight
17 Rotation along horizontal axis

- An aeronautical map that provides interesting patterns for the manufacturers of children's curtains.

Chock:

- Sudden and usually unpleasant surprise suffered by pilots in Mexico.
- Pieces of wood the line boy slips in front of the wheels while the pilot isn't looking.

"Clear:" Warning shouted two seconds after hitting the starter button. [18]

Cockpit:

- A confined space in which two chickens fight each other, especially when they can't find the airport in a rainstorm.
- Area in which the pilot sits while attempting to figure out where he is.

Collision: Unplanned contact between one aircraft and another. As a rule, collisions that result in the creation of several smaller and less airworthy pieces of the original two is thought to be the most serious.

Cone of Confusion: An area about the size of New Jersey, located near the final approach beacon at an airport.

Control Tower: A small shack on stilts inhabited by government pensioners who can't hear. When they become blind, they are sent to Centers.

Course: Popular alternate landing field marked by fairways and greens. Curiously, pilots who land here are said to be "off-course."

Crab:

- A technique used by pilots to compensate for crosswinds, usually without success.

---

18 Warning that the propeller is about to turn very fast.

- Pilot who has just ground-looped[19] after trying unsuccessfully to use this technique.
- Pilot who has been unsuccessful in finding a suitable landing site (also see "Suitable Landing Site"). [20]

Crash:

- To bed down for the night.
- What every pilot hopes not to do once he has found a suitable landing site.

Dead Reckoning: You reckon correctly or you are.[21]

De-icer: De person dat takes de ice off de wings.

Dive: Pilot's lounge or airport cafe.

Drag Chute: Emergency escape slide near co-pilot's window. Opens automatically if eccentric male captain shows up in women's clothes. [22]

Engine Failure: A condition that occurs when all fuel tanks become filled with air.

Exceptional Flying Ability: Has equal number of takeoffs and landings.

FAA: Fear And Alarm [23]

Fast: Describes the speed of any high-performance aircraft. Lower-performance and training aircraft are described as "half-fast."

Final Approach:

- Last pass a pilot makes at the opposite sex before giving up.
- Many a seasoned pilot's last landing.
- Many a student pilot's first landing.

---

19 Sharp, uncontrollable turn while on the ground.
20 Aircraft angle to compensate for cross-winds
21 Estimating position with limited information
22 Parachute installed on some aircraft to assist in deceleration
23 Federal Aviation Administration

Flight Attendant: A pretty gal who asks you what you want, then straps you in so you can't get it.

Flight Instructor: Individual of dubious reputation, paid vast sums of money to impart knowledge of questionable value and to cast serious doubt on the coordination, intelligence and ancestry of student pilots.

Flight Plan: Scheme to get away from home to go flying.

Glide Distance: Half the distance from an airplane to the nearest emergency landing field.

Glider: Formerly "airplane," before running out of fuel.

Grass Strip: Often performed by exotic female flight attendants while enroute to Hawaii.

Gross Weight:

- A 350-pound pilot (also see "Split S").
- Maximum permissible takeoff weight plus two suitcases, ten cans of oil, four sleeping bags, four rifles, ammo, eight cases of beer, and the groceries.

Hangar: Home for anything that flies, mostly birds.

Heated Air Mass: Usually found near hangar, flight lounge, airport cafe or attractive, non-flying members of the opposite sex.

Holding Pattern: The term applied to the dogfight in progress over the airspace serving a terminal airport.

Horizontally Opposed: *No!* (Also see "Arctic Frost")[24]

Jet-assisted Takeoff:

- A rapid-takeoff procedure used by a general aviation pilot who suddenly finds himself taking off on a runway directly in front of a departing 747.
- Takeoff by pilot who ordered enchiladas for lunch at the airport coffee shop. [25]

---

24 Pistons directly opposite
25 Rocket assisted takeoff

Kilometer: A unit of measurement used on charts to further confuse pilots who already have trouble with knots.

Lean Mixture: Non-alcoholic beer. [26]

Log: A small rectangular notebook used by pilots to record lies.

Magneto:

- Spanish for, "What a cool-looking magnet!"
- Not-very-famous Italian vaudeville magician, "The Great Magneto." [27]

Mini Maglite: Device designed to support the AA battery industry.

Motor: A word used by Englishmen and student pilots when referring to an aircraft engine. (Also see "Aerodrome")

Nanosecond: Time delay between the Low Fuel Warning light and fuel not reaching the carburetor.

Navigation: The process by which a pilot finds his way from point A to point B while actually trying to get to point C.

Oshkosh: A town in Wisconsin that's the site of the annual Experimental Aircraft Association fly-in. Is believed to have been named after the sound that most experimental aircraft engines make.

Parasitic Drag: A pilot who bums a ride in back, then complains about the service. [28]

Pitch: The story you give your wife about needing an airplane to use in your business. [29]

Pitot Tube: On long flights, something into which the pilot can pitot. [30]

---

26 High percentage of air to fuel
27 Part of ignition system
28 Caused by non-lifting components such as fixed landing gear.
29 Angle of propeller blades
30 Measures air speed

Prop Wash:
- Cleaning agent used by student pilots.
- Pilots' equivalent of "hogwash." [31]

Pylon: All aboard! [32]

Radar: An extremely realistic type of video game, often found at airports. Players try to send small game-pieces, called "blips," from one side of the screen to the other without colliding with each other. Player with the fewest collisions wins. [33]

Range: Usually about three miles short of the destination.

Roger:
- The most popular name in radio.
- Used when you're not sure what else to say. [34]

Runway:
- Place where exotic flight attendant starts her act (also see "Airstrip").
- Ramp extending from the stage into the audience area at all good burlesque houses in Vegas.

Safety Belt: Drink taken by instructor before flying with difficult student.

Sectional[35] Chart: Any chart that ends 25 nm[36] short of your destination.

Short-field Takeoff: A takeoff from any field less than 10,000 feet long.

Skin Drag: Costume party in San Francisco.[37]

Slip: Apparel worn by some pilots.[38]

---

31 Current of air caused by propeller or rotor
32 Turning point in an aircraft race
33 Radio Detection and Ranging
34 Transmission understood
35 Air map
36 Nautical miles
37 Air friction
38 Sideways maneuver to quickly lose altitude

Split S: What happens to the pants of overweight pilots (also see "Gross Weight"). [39]

Spoilers: The Federal Aviation Administration. [40]

Stall: Technique used to explain to the bank why your car payment is late because you spent the money on flying.

Steep Bank: Banks that charge pilots more than 10% interest.

Suitable Landing Site: An attractive member of the opposite sex. Suitability may sometimes be affected by Arctic Frost.

Taildragger: An old pilot after a long flight. [41]

Tailwind: Results from eating beans in the airport coffee shop. Often causes oxygen deficiency in the immediate vicinity.

Up! Up!: A appeal used by pilots taking off from Colorado Springs.

Walkaround: What you do when waiting for weather to clear. [42]

Wilco: Roger's brother, the nerd. [43]

Windsock: Well-perforated item of clothing worn inside the shoe by underpaid co-pilot who can't afford a replacement or a darning needle. [44]

Wingstrut: Peculiar, ritualistic walk performed by student pilots upon getting out of low-winged trainers following first flight performed without instructor yelling at them. Usually results in instructor yelling at them. [45]

Yankee: Any pilot who asks Houston tower to "Say again."

Zero: Style and artistry points earned for a gear-up landing.

---

39 Air combat maneuver
40 Hinged plate on top of wing to reduce lift when raised
41 Main wheels under wings. Smaller wheel at rear of fuselage. Sits nose up.
42 Will comply with instructions
43 Shows wind direction in small airport
44 Support for wing on small airport
45 Post-flight inspection

ATIS – Automatic Terminal Information System

In aviation, routine information concerning a large airport such as altimeter reading, runway conditions, wind direction and speed, the ceiling, and special conditions are recorded and broadcast so that pilots may be aware of the general situation without live voice transmission from the Tower. Since these are recorded every hour, each new recording is identified with a different phonetic letter of the alphabet. This letter is represented by the appropriate word.

For example: Alpha is for A, Bravo is for B, Charlie represents C and so on.

The tower may ask if the flight has the particular transmission as below. The pilot may say, "With (whatever the current ATIS transmission is) such as 'Tango' meaning the letter T. "With Tango" is the expression. Or "do you have Tango?"

Tower: "XX Air, do you have Charlie?"

XX Air: "Tower, XX Air, Negative. We left him back at the hanger!"

Tower: "XX Air, do you have Echo?"

XX Air: "Tower, XX Air, Negative. Receiving you loud and clear."

Tower: "XX Air, do you have Hotel?"

XX Air: "Tower, XX Air, Negative. We're staying with friends."

Tower: "XX Air, do you have Juliet?"

XX Air: "Tower, Affirmative, but please don't say anything to my wife."

Tower: "XX Air, do you have Kilo?"

XX Air: "Tower, XX Air, Negative. But I think there a couple of roaches in the ashtray!"

Tower: "XX Air, do you have Mike?"
XX Air: "Tower, XX Air, Negative. I have a push-to-talk button and a headset!"

Tower: "XX Air, do you have Oscar?
XX Air: "Tower, XX Air, Negative, but I'm expecting a nomination this year!"

Tower: "XX Air, do you have Papa?"
XX Air: "Tower, XX Air, Negative. But I wrote him a letter last week!"

Tower: "XX Air, do you have Romeo?"
XX Air: "Tower, XX Air, Negative, Negative! Wherefore art thou, Romeo?"

Tower: "XX Air, do you have Uniform?"
XX Air: "Tower, XX Air, Negative. Just jeans and sweatshirt."

Tower: "XX Air, do you have Victor?"
XX Air: "Tower, XX Air, Negative. Who's Victor?"

Tower: "XX Air, do you have Xray?"
XX Air: "Tower, XX Air, Negative. My doctor wants a CAT Scan."

Tower: "XX Air, do you have Whiskey?"
XX Air: "Tower, XX Air, Negative, not in last eight hours. Am I not on assigned heading?

— Bill Turcotte

"San Carlos airport information Zulu. Bird advisory in effect; 150 foot crane[46] one mile southwest of the airport."

While working as a volunteer at our local Boy Scout Council office, one of the professional staff, who was wearing street clothes instead of her usual uniform, was talking about the International Phonetic Alphabet. She said that she had learned it some years ago and proceeded to recite it. "Alpha, Bravo, Charlie, Delta, etc." But, when she got to the letter "U," she stumbled and asked for help.

I offered a hint: "What aren't you wearing today?"

"Underwear?" she replied.

---

46 Obviously recorded by a joker.

TWELVE

Flight Training

WEEK 1

Monday: Rain

Tuesday: Rain

Wednesday: No rain. No visibility either.

Thursday: Take instructor to lunch. Discover I don't know enough to take instructor to lunch.

Friday: Fly! Did first stall; second stall during same maneuver. Cover instructor with lunch.

WEEK 2

Monday: Learned not to scrape frost off plexiglass with ice-scraper. Used big scratch as marker to set pitch[47].

Tuesday: Instructor wants me to stop calling throttle, *"That Big Knob Thing."* Also hates when I call instruments, *"gadgets."*

Wednesday: Radios won't pick up radio stations, so I turned them off. Instructor seems to think I missed something.

Thursday: Learned ten degree bank is not a steep turn. Did stall again today. Lost 2000 feet. Instructor said that was some kind of record. My first compliment.

---

47 Propeller blade angle

Friday: Did steep turn. Instructor said I wasn't ready for inverted flight yet.

WEEK 3

Monday: Instructor called in sick. New instructor told me to stop calling her, "Babe." Did steep turns. She said I had to have permission for inverted flight.

Tuesday: Instructor back. He told me to stop calling him "Babe," too. He got mad when I pulled power back on takeoff because the engine was too loud.

Wednesday: Instructor said, after the first twenty hours, most students have established a learning curve. He said there's a slight bend in mine. Aha, progress!

Thursday: Did stalls. Clean recovery. Instructor said I did good job. Also did turns around a point. Instructor warned me never to pick ex-fiancé's house as the point again.

Friday: Did pattern work. Instructor said that if downwind, base, and final formed a triangle, I'd be perfect. More praise!

WEEK 4

Monday: First landing at a controlled field. Did fine until I told the captain in the 747 ahead of us on the taxiway to move his bird. Instructor says we'll have ground school all this week on radio procedures.

Tuesday: Asked instructor if everyone in his family had turned gray at such an early age. He smiled. We did takeoff stalls. He says I did just fine, but to wait until we reached altitude next time.

Wednesday: Flew through clouds. I thought those radio towers were a lot lower. I'm sure my instructor is going gray.

Thursday: Left flaps down for entire flight. Instructor asked why. I told him I wanted the extra lift as a safety margin. More ground school.

Friday: Asked instructor when I could solo. I've never seen anyone actually laugh until they cried before.

A student was having difficulty with his landings. Seems like he would bounce it in every time. However, on the first night lesson, the student greased all of his landings.

Puzzled, the instructor asked, "How are you doing that? You have so much trouble during the day?"

The student replied, "It's easy. I continue the approach until you stiffen up, then I just pull back."

Student and instructor are on a dual[48], night cross-country. Instructor turns down the panel lights, "Okay, you've just lost your lights. What are you going to do?"

Student pulls out a flashlight. "I get out my flashlight."

Instructor grabs flashlight. "The batteries are dead. Now what are you going to do?"

Student pulls out another flashlight. "I get out my other flashlight."

Instructor grabs next flashlight. "The bulb is burned out on this one. Now what?"

Student pulls out yet a third flashlight. "I use this flashlight."

Instructor grabs this one too. "*All* your flashlights are dead. Now what?"

"I use this glow stick."

"Sighhhhhh. Just fly the plane without any lights, Okay?"

---

48 Dual controls

The photographer for a national magazine was assigned to get photos of a great forest fire. Smoke at the scene was too thick to get any good shots, so he frantically called his home office to hire a plane.

"It'll be waiting for you at the airport!" he was assured by his editor.

As soon as he got to the small, rural airport, sure enough, a plane was warming up near the runway. He jumped in with his equipment and yelled, "Let's go! Let's go!" The pilot swung the plane into the wind. Soon they were in the air.

"Fly over the north side of the fire," said the photographer, "and make three or four low level passes."

"Why?" asked the pilot.

"Because I'm going to take pictures! I'm a photographer, and photographers take pictures!" said the photographer with great exasperation.

After a long pause the pilot said, "You mean you're not the instructor?"

A few years ago while sitting in a local FBO[49] office, I was watching a lone student doing touch and gos. It was a real quiet Sunday afternoon, and there was no other airplane traffic. The student would call, "Bowman tower, Piper 1234 on final for touch and go."

But when he touched, he would bounce three or four times before he applied power to go around (take off again). After about five or six times of this the tower finally said, "Piper 1234 cleared for a touch and a touch and a touch and a go...."

— Al Isley

---

49 Flight Service Center

Tower: "Aircraft on final, go around aircraft on runway."

Solo student pilot: "Roger" (continues descent.)

Tower: "Aircraft, *Go Around.*"

Student: "Roger" (continues descent.)

Tower: (Screaming) "*Aircraft, Go Around!*"

Student: "Roger" (continues descent.)

So, the student pilot plunks his airplane down on the numbers, taxies up to where the twin is sitting in the middle of the runway, *goes around it,* and continues to the taxiway.

A seventy-year-old, experienced flight instructor had to go to a "new" FAA medical examiner since he had outlived the previous AME[50]. Try as he could, the "rookie" AME could find no medical faults with the wise old silver-haired flight instructor except for a slightly red eye. Inquiring into this problem, the AME asked how long the eye had been red, and did it hurt, etc.

"It's been red for two weeks, but much better now, and it never hurts when I fly."

"I understand, but have you ever had a purulent (pus) discharge?"

"Not me, Doc. I'm flat footed and was always 4-F."

I was flying my first "Bay Tour" in the San Francisco Bay area and didn't yet know many of the landmarks. As I continued up the coastline I was handed over to SFO, who announced, "Cessna 9876, turn left to 300 and report shoreline."

I promptly reported that I was "unable." That course wouldn't take me over the Shoreline Amphitheater. The landmark was retreating behind me.

Regardless, the controller stated that it was at my 12:00, and "please report shoreline." After going back and forth a

---

50 Aviation Medical Examiner

few times, the controller said, a bit exasperatedly, "It's the long thing made of sand."

As part of a private pilot ground-school curriculum, I take my students on a tour of the Deer Valley (Ariz.) Control Tower. During one recent tour, the two controllers on duty happened to be women. As one began her introduction, she said, "The first thing we want you to notice is that this is an unmanned facility."

Student pilot: "I'm lost; I'm over a lake and heading toward the big E (East)."

Controller: "Make several ninety degree turns so I can identify you on radar." (short pause)

Controller: "Okay then. That lake is the Atlantic Ocean. Suggest you turn to the big W immediately."

When often asked how much it costs to learn how to fly, we've just as often replied, "About a hundred bucks. Learning how to land will cost you $4,500."

It's the day of my first solo flight, and the only member of my family who could show up to watch was my grandmother. Grandma is no stranger to aviation. Her first husband was a B-26 pilot shot down in WWII. So I'm out to do my solo. Grandma is on the porch at the flight school, surrounded by all the CFI[51]s and students.

The crowd on the porch is discussing whether or not the weather is going to stay good enough for cross-country flying, as there are many towering cumulus clouds[52] building. They'd

---

51 Certified Flight Instructor
52 Mother of thunderstorms

consulted the NEXRAD[53] in the school's weather room. They'd called the FSS. They'd solicited PIREPs[54] from returning pilots.

Grandma, hearing all this, decides to put her opinion into the mix. "It's not going to rain," she announces. "My bones aren't hurting."

Whereupon all the pilots on the porch immediately decided to go flying.

Instructor (briefing student for his first dual cross-country): "What would you do if I fell unconscious halfway through the trip?"

Student: "Uh, let's see…. Complete the flight, then log it as half dual and half solo?"

The student pilot radioed for taxi instructions, sounding pretty nervous. When the Tower asked if he was departing VFR[55], or IFR[56] or his reply was:

"No, I'm G.I. Bill."

This CFI and his student are holding on the runway for departing cross traffic when suddenly a deer runs out of the nearby woods, stops in the middle of the runway, and just stands there looking at them.

Tower: "Cessna 229 cleared for take-off."

Student: "What should I do? What should I do?"

Instructor: "What do you think you should do?"

Student: (think-think-think) "Maybe if I taxi toward him, it'll scare him away."

Instructor: "That's a good idea."

---

53 National weather surveillance radar
54 National Weather Service for Aviation
55 Visual Flight Rules
56 Instrument Flight Rules

Student taxies toward deer, but deer is macho and holds position.

Tower: "Cessna 229 cleared for take-off, runway 29."

Student: "What should I do? What should I do?"

Instructor: "What do you think you should do?"

Student: (think-think-think) "Maybe I should tell the tower."

Instructor: "That's a good idea."

Student: "Cessna 229, uh, there's a deer down here on the runway. (long pause)

Tower: "Roger 229, hold your position. Deer on runway 29 cleared for immediate departure." (Two seconds, and I presume by coincidence, the deer bolts from the runway and runs back into the woods.)

Tower: "Cessna 229 cleared for departure, runway 29. Caution wake turbulence[57], departing deer."

Excerpt From FAA Accident Report, Eyewitness Statement
Aircraft: Cessna 172
Pilot: 30 Yrs Old, CFI, IR[58]
Fatalities: None
Damage: Substantial
Date of Accident: July 10, 1982
Witness: Line attendant at airport

Pilot came to airport at 9 AM, 10 Jul 1982. Line boy reports padlock on his hangar door was so rusted he had to break it off with a 10# ball-peen hammer.

Also had to inflate all three tires and scrape pigeon droppings off wind-screen. After several attempts to drain fuel strainers, pilot finally got what looked like fuel out of the wing's

---

57 Wake turbulence caused by large departing aircraft.
58 Instrument Rated

sumps. Couldn't get the oil dipstick out of the engine, but pilot said it was okay last time he looked.

Engine started okay; ran rough for about 1/2 minute, then died. Next, battery would not turn prop. Used battery cart and, although starter was smoking real good, it finally started. The prop wash blew the smoke away.

Line boy offered to fuel airplane up, but pilot said he was late for an appointment at a nearby airport. Said it wasn't far. Taxied about 1/2 way out to active runway. The engine stopped. Pushed it back to the fuel pumps and bought three gallons for the left wing tank. Started it again. This time, he was almost out to the runway when it quit again. Put a little rock under nose wheel; hand propped[59] it; and was seen still trying to climb in the airplane as it went across the runway. Finally got in it; blew out the right tire trying to stop before the cement plant.

When he taxied back in to have the tire changed, he also had the line boy hit the right wing with three gallons of gas. Witness, who saw the take-off, said the aircraft lined up and took off to the north. Takeoff looked fairly normal. Nose came up about 300 ft down the runway. At midfield, the nose came down. Engine coughed twice. Pilot then cut power and applied the brakes, which made both doors fly open.

After several real loud run-ups at the end, he turned her around and took off in the other direction going south into the wind. Only this time he horsed her off at the end and pulled her up real steep to about 300 feet like one of them jet fighter planes. Then the engine quit!

Did sort of a slow turn back toward the airport. At about 30 feet from the McDonald's café, she started roaring again. He did sort of a high speed pass down the runway, put the flaps

---

59 Start motor by turning propeller manually.

down to full, and that sucker went up like he was going to do an Immelman[60]!

The engine quit again. He turned right. I thought he was coming right through the front window of the F.B.O., but he pulled her up, went through the TV antenna and the little rooster with the NSE&W things, over the building then bounced the main wheels off the roof of three different cars in the lot; a Porsche, a Mercedes, and Dr. Brown's new Eldorado.

When he bounced off the Eldorado, the engine roared to life, and he got her flying again. Came around toward the runway and set her down; once on the overrun, once on the runway, and once in the grass beside the runway. He taxied into the ramp, shut her down and ordered three more gallons of gas. Said it was for safety's sake.

Then he asked where the phone booth was so he could call his flying student to tell him he was going to be a little bit late.

Early in my flying career, I had my first night flight. Looking down in the darkness, I asked my instructor what we'd do if the engine failed. "Get the plane gliding in a controlled descent, attempt to restart the engine, and make a Mayday call," he explained. "The only difference between day and night flying is that the terrain below won't be clearly visible, so the aircraft should be headed toward whatever looks most like a clear area, and it should be approaching into the wind. Conserve the battery, turn on the landing light when you get close to the ground, and if you like what you see, land."

"All right, but what if I don't like what I see?"

My instructor gave me a compassionate look in the dim cockpit, and said softly, "Turn off the landing light."

---

60 Acrobatic maneuver

Student pilot: (who forgot to ask for surface wind) "Please pass wind."

Lost student pilot: "Unknown airport with Cessna 150 circling overhead, identify yourself."

The venerable Cessna 152 manual recommends testing the stall warning horn by placing a clean cloth over the stall vent and drawing a vacuum. When an instructor asked a student at our club how to test the stall warning horn, he replied, "Place your mouth over the wing stall vent and suck hard till the siren goes off."

The instructor then asked, "What would you do if the vent was full of bugs and such?"

The student pondered for a moment, then replied, "Ask the instructor to place his mouth over the wing stall vent and suck hard till the siren goes off."

During night ops training the instructor wanted to simulate a landing light failure.

Tower: "Cessna 1234, cleared to land Runway 31."

Pilot: "Cleared to land, Cessna 1234. We'll switch off the landing light for training purposes."

Tower: "Roger. Do you want us to switch off the runway lights as well?"

— Horst Schneider

Ground Controller: "Cessna calling ground control. Are you a Skymaster?[61]"

Pilot's reply: "No, Sir. I'm just a student pilot."

— Philip Bridges, pdb1@ae.msstate.edu

---

61 A model of Cessna

A student pilot had an engine failure one day. He successfully landed and found his way to a phone to call the club house. He gave his position to his instructor, who said he would pop straight out in one of the club's aircraft to pick him up.

The instructor found the downed student, parked in a rather small looking field. "Hmmm, if he can get in there, so can I!"

He performed a textbook short field landing and parked neatly in the hedge at the far end of the field.

On extricating himself from the brambles, he asked the student how on earth he had managed to land in such a confined space. "Oh, I didn't. I landed in that big field over there and pushed the plane in here to give you more room."

— Andy Cullington, andy.cullington@gecm.com

After completing a flight lesson for the day, I asked my instructor if he could give my twelve-year-old son his first ride in an airplane. Thanks to my CFI[62] being a genuine promoter of general aviation (and a good friend), my son got his first ride in the left seat.

After landing, my CFI asked him how he liked the ride, to which my son exclaimed, "Wow! Just like the flight simulator on my computer, only the graphics are a whole lot better!"

The young student pilot was flying with an examiner for the first time. The examiner said, "Why don't we start with something simple like straight and level?"

The student pilot replied, "Okay, which do you want first?"

---

62 Certified Flight Instructor

At one point, we were all primary students, understanding little, questioning even less, but placing complete faith in our instructor. Many of the little things necessary to get through the first few lessons before solo were done by rote, without a great deal of understanding, such as ensuring anyone on the ground near the airplane was aware the prop was about to spin.

One instructor was working with a pre-solo student. Instead of using the phrase, "Clear prop!" before turning the key, the instructor had simply taught his pupil to use the word "Clear!" presumably shouted loudly enough that those inside the FBO could hear.

Of course, students rarely fly in poor weather. But one day, preflight complete, the student reached for the key, looked outside the airplane, and shouted, "Cloudy!"

— Avflash

THIRTEEN

Pilots

ABOUT PILOTS

The average pilot, despite the sometimes swaggering exterior, is very much capable of such feelings as love, affection, intimacy and caring. These feelings just don't involve anyone else.

What's the difference between a pilot and a pig?
The pig doesn't turn into a pilot after six beers.

What's the difference between God and pilots?
God doesn't think he's a pilot.

Then there's the pilot who dies and goes to heaven. While waiting to check in he notices a large twin[63] coming in high-and-hot[64] to a nearby landing strip.

The twin pilot blows the landing, collapses the nose gear, strikes the props[65]; then gets out and walks away.

Fifteen minutes later, same scene: another twin, another blown landing. Same guy gets out of the wrecked plane.

63 Two motors
64 Too high, too fast
65 Tips hit ground

The fellow waiting to check in to heaven is amazed. He turns to St. Peter and says, "What's the story with the twin pilot over there?"

"Oh, that's just God," says St. Peter. "He thinks he's a surgeon."

Definition of a pilot: The first one to arrive at the scene of an aircraft accident.

Trust your captain, but keep your seat belt securely fastened anyway.

There are many excellent pilots who would rather do anything than land a private airplane at Newark, Cleveland, or Chicago.

— *Aviation* magazine, August 1935.

I used to be an airline pilot. I got fired because I kept locking the keys in the plane. They caught me on an eighty foot stepladder with a coat hanger.

A pilot friend of mine was at a private game reserve near South Africa's Kruger Park. After dinner, the guests had assembled around the campfire for nightcaps and general chatter. Our intrepid aviator was regaling the guests endlessly with stories of his heroism behind the controls of an aircraft, explaining why pilots are such a special breed of human beings.

One of the guests was a middle-aged, experienced, senior cabin attendant with a major airline on a stopover in South Africa. She had obviously come across every type of pilot in her time, including the sort now lecturing the guests. When the monologue finished, she spoke up, "That was great! Tell me, do you know what they call little eagles?"

"Eaglets," my friend replied.

"Right. And what about little pigs?"

"Piglets," came the confident response.

"You bet. How about little owls?"

No problem. "Owlets."

"Yup. Say, do you know what they call little hemorrhoids?" No reply. My friend confessed he didn't know.

"Pilots," said the hostie.

With that she bade everyone goodnight and went to bed!

— Graham Speller, speller@iaccess.za

How do you know when you're halfway through a date with a pilot?

When he says, "That's enough about flying; let's talk about me!"

Have you ever been on a plane and seen some uniformed pilots sitting in the passenger cabin? This is not at all uncommon, since most airlines at one time or another need pilots to cover a flight at an airport other than the one at which they're based. When pilots ride this way as passengers, this is known in the industry as "deadheading." In some cases, due to weather, mechanical problems, or crew flight-time legalities, crews are called out at the last moment to catch a deadheading flight. And so begins our story.

While taxiing out for takeoff, the Boeing 727 suddenly came to a stop. With the aircraft still on the taxiway, the flight attendant in the back began to lower the aft stairway. Behind the plane, a van with flashing lights came to a screeching halt and out jumped three deadheading pilots. They grabbed their bags and ran to the plane.

As they ran up the stairs, the pilot in front continued running up the aisle shouting, "I can't believe the flight attendant got the plane this far. I didn't know she even knew how to start the engines!"

For some of the passengers, it took quite a while before they realized they had been had. The looks on their faces was a hoot.

WHY I WANT TO BE A PILOT

When I grow up, I want to be a pilot because it's a fun job and easy to do. That's why there are so many pilots flying around these days.

Pilots don't need much school. They just have to learn to read numbers so they can read their instruments. I guess they should be able to read a road map, too.

Pilots should be brave so they won't get scared if it's foggy and they can't see, or if a wing or motor falls off. Pilots have to have good eyes to see through the clouds, and they can't be afraid of thunder or lightning because they're much closer to them than we are.

The salary pilots make is another thing I like. They make more money than they know what to do with. This is because most people think that flying a plane is dangerous, except pilots don't because they know how easy it is.

I hope I don't get airsick because I get carsick and, if I get airsick, I couldn't be a pilot. Then I would have to go to work.

— purported to have been written by a
fifth grade student at Jefferson School, Beaufort, SC.
First published in the *South Carolina Aviation News*

YOU KNOW YOU ARE A PILOT WHEN:

You turn on your car radio and expect to hear the ATIS.

Before you start your car, you reach for your checklist.

When you start going downhill in your car, you check the dash for the Attitude Indicator.

When the road is long and straight, you're tempted to drive the centerline[66].

When your normal talking voice starts sounding like an Air Traffic Controller.

When you start looking for the lean knob (fuel mixture) on your car's instrument panel.

An airline pilot rear-ended a car in front of him while driving home from work one night.

He told the traffic court judge that it was late, he was tired, and when he saw the car ahead and realized he couldn't stop in time, he slammed on the gas and pulled back on the steering wheel, fully expecting to go up and over.

Verdict: unknown.

During the "rush hour" at Houston's Hobby Airport, a flight was delayed due to a mechanical problem.

Since they needed the gate for another flight, the aircraft was backed away from the gate while the maintenance crew worked on it. The passengers were then told the new gate number, which was some distance away. Everyone moved to the new gate, only to find a third gate had been designated for them.

After some further shuffling, everyone got on board, and as they were settling in, the flight attendant made the standard announcement, "We apologize for the inconvenience of this last-minute gate change. This flight is going to Washington, D.C. If your destination is not Washington, D.C., then you should deplane at this time."

---

66 As the middle of a runway

A confused-looking and red-faced pilot emerged from the cockpit, carrying his bags. "Sorry," he said, "Wrong plane."

Taxiing down the tarmac, the jetliner abruptly stopped, turned around, and returned to the gate. After an hour-long wait, it finally took off.

A concerned passenger asked the flight attendant, "What was the problem?"

"The pilot was bothered by a noise he heard in the engine," he explained. "It took us awhile to find another pilot."

An airliner takes off from Newark airport. The pilot announces, "Thanks for flying with us, etc. We'll be cruising at 35,000 ft, etc." Then, thinking the mike was off, he says to the co-pilot, "I'm going to take a dump. Then I'm gonna nail that new flight attendant." The mike was still hot. Everyone on board heard.

One of the flight attendants is aghast at hearing this and rushes forward to shut the pilot up.

An old lady says to her, "No need to run, Dearie. He has to take a dump first."

TOP TEN SIGNS THAT YOU'RE AN AVIATION ADDICT:
You speed dial ATIS.

You whine and fret on every nice day that you're not up in the air.

You whine and fret every day that the wx[67] is too bad for flying.

You get a wx briefing on days you can't fly, just to see if the wx is really as nice for flying as it looks.

---

67 Abbreviation for weather

You get a briefing on days with awful wx, just to assure yourself that the wx really would be too bad to fly.

You learn mental methods for flight planning, and spend boring meetings planning flying trips.

You calculate every expenditure in terms of flight hours (fifty cents at the candy machine every day is 0.01 flight hours).

Your girlfriend is made of aluminum. Her name starts with an "N[68]".

You get in your car and find that it drives itself to the airport.

You become an instructor so you can be paid to go for airplane rides.

WAYS TO TELL IF YOUR PILOT IS ON DRUGS:

All the in-flight meals are missing their dessert squares.

Between "May I" and "have your attention", there's a 45-second pause.

He's constantly yelling, "Take that, Red Baron!"

Shuttle from New York to Boston includes stopover in Colombia.

For the last hour, he's been riding the beverage cart like a rodeo cowboy.

Keeps coming on the P.A. to point out clouds that look like his old high school teachers.

When you fly over International Date Line, he yells, "Dude! We're, like, time traveling!"

When he exhales, the oxygen masks drop.

YOU MIGHT BE A FREIGHT DOG[69] IF:

Your airplane was getting old when you were born.

You haven't done a daylight landing in the past six months.

---

68 Non-commercial
69 Freighter pilot

ATC[70] advises you of smoother air at a different altitude, and you don't care.

When you taxi up to an FBO they roll out the red carpet, but quickly take it back when they recognize you.

You call the hotel van for pick up, and they don't understand where you are on the airport.

Center asks you to "keep the chickens down" so they can hear you talk.

Your airplane has more than 75,000 cycles.

Your company call sign is "Oil Can."

The lady at the FBO locks up the popcorn machine because you plan on "making a meal of it."

Your airplane has more than eight faded logos on it.

You wear the same shirt for a week and no one complains.

Center mispronounces your call sign more than three times in one flight.

Your boss mysteriously jacks up your max takeoff weight during the holiday season.

Every FBO makes you park out of sight of their building.

You've ever walked barefoot through the FBO because you just woke up.

You mark every ramp with engine oil.

Everything you own is in your flight bag and suitcase.

— David Sipe, djsipe@hsonline.net

YOU KNOW YOU'RE A REDNECK PILOT IF:

If you have ever responded in the affirmative to ATC with the phrase "That's a big 10-4!"

If you typically answer female controllers with titles like "sugar" or "little darlin'."

---

70 Air Traffic Control

If you have ever used a relief tube as a spittoon.

You've retro-fitted a gun rack in your Cessna 172.

Your stall warning plays "Dixie."

Your cross-country flight plan uses flea markets as checkpoints.

You think sectional charts should show trailer parks.

You've ever hauled lumber in your plane.

You've ever used moonshine as Avgas[71].

Your toothpick keeps poking your mike.

You've ever just taxied around the airport drinking beer.

You've ever fantasized of flying with Dolly Parton in your airplane.

You've ever bought pilot supplies at a flea market.

You wouldn't be caught dead in a Grumman Yankee.

You use a Purina feed sack for a wind sock.

The side of your airplane has a sign advertising your septic tank service.

You think GPS stands for Gators Play Seminoles.

You refer to formation flying as "we got us a convoy."

Your matched set of luggage is three grocery bags from Piggly Wiggly[72].

You've ever fueled your airplane from a mason jar.

You have more than one roll of duct tape holding your cowling[73] together.

Your preflight includes removing all of the clover, grass, and wheat from your landing gear.

You siphon gas from your tractor to put in your airplane.

You've never landed at an actual airport though you've been flying for years.

---

71 Aviation gas
72 Grocery chain
73 Metal covering an aircraft engine

You consider anything over 100 feet AGL[74] to be high altitude flight.

There are parts of your airplane labeled John Deere.

You've never actually seen a sectional (map), but have all of the Texaco road maps for your flying area.

There's exhaust residue on the right side of your aircraft and tobacco stains on the left.

You have fuzzy dice hanging from the magnetic compass.

You put hay in the baggage compartment so your dogs don't get cold.

Your weight and balance calculations include five cases of Budweiser®.

There are grass stains on your propeller tips.

Somewhere on your airplane is an *I'd Rather Be Fishing* bumper sticker.

You navigate with your ADF[75] tuned exclusively to country stations.

You have Mack mud flaps behind your main wheels.

You have to buzz the strip to chase off all the sheep.

You've landed on the main street of your town for a cup of coffee.

You fly to family reunions to meet girls.

You've ever tried to pick up girls at Oshkosh[76].

The spittoon is wedged between the rudder pedals.

You have a Cessna 150 up on cement blocks in your front yard.

You keep a spare pack of Skoal[77] in the plane.

Your bass boat has more horsepower than your plane's engine.

---

74 Above Ground Level
75 Automatic Direction Finder
76 Wisconsin home of National Experimental Aircraft Fly-in
77 Chewing tobacco

You've ever referred to your horizontal stabilizer as "the tailgate. "

You have tobacco stains on your empennage[78].

You're wondering what the hell is an empennage? "

You think ZULU[79] time means something to do with Africa.

You think "Ultralite[80]" is a new beer from Budweiser.

You have a Confederate flag on your comm. antenna.

You use your parachute to cover your plane.

The tread pattern, if any, on your main tires don't match.

Just before the crash, everybody at the airport heard you say, "Hey, y'all; watch this!"

A pilot is flying a small, single-engine charter plane with a couple of important execs on board into Seattle airport. The fog is so thick that visibility is only forty feet. His instruments are out. He circles, looking for a landmark.

After an hour, he's low on fuel and his passengers are very nervous. At last, through a small opening in the fog, he sees a tall building with one guy working alone on the fifth floor.

Circling, the pilot banks and shouts through his open window, "Hi, where am I?"

The solitary office worker replies, "You're in an airplane."

The pilot executes a swift 275 degree turn and makes a perfect blind landing on the airport's runway five miles away. Just as the plane stops, the engines cough and die from lack of fuel. The stunned passengers are relieved and ask the pilot how he did it.

"Simple," replies the pilot, "I asked the guy in that building a simple question. The answer he gave me was 100% correct, but absolutely useless. Therefore, that must have been the Microsoft

---

78 Aircraft tail assembly
79 Coordinated Universal Time
80 Little sport aircraft

Excel support office. I know that from there, the airport is three minutes away on a heading of 87 degrees."

While boarding a coast-to-coast flight with his two boys, a pilot asked the captain if he could show the kids where Dad worked. The captain said, "Sure, come on in." He and the F/O[81] demo'd all the bells and whistles for the kids, then got back to work.

The kids watched as the captain pulled out his charts and began to highlight the planned route. The seven-year-old was amazed by this and asked quietly, "Dad, what's he doing?"

Before Dad could respond, his nine-year-old brother answered, "What do you think he's doing? He's coloring."

I want to die peacefully in my sleep like my grandfather; not screaming in terror, like his passengers.

Being a relatively new pilot, I've always been very enthusiastic and felt that my wife may have been growing weary of all the "pilot talk." However, it was a gorgeous fall day. A perfect opportunity for the "$100 hamburger," so at her suggestion, we flew out enjoying beautiful foliage scenery all the way.

As we dined at the restaurant, we were suddenly visited by a persistent fly that seemed intent on staying for the full meal. After swatting at it a time or two, I could no longer see it when my wife informed me, "Honey, I think he departed the pattern[82] to the north."

A male pilot is a confused soul who talks about women when he's flying, and about flying when he's with a woman.

---

81 First Officer
82 Flight pattern

There's always some "joker" who asks loudly as I (a pilot) am sitting down in the back of the airplane: "Aren't you supposed to be up front?"

Well, one time I responded loud enough for everyone to hear. "This is one of the newest airplanes in the world. It's totally computerized. I'm onboard just in case something goes wrong so I can reset the computer."

I had a nice visit with my parents in Florida and, as usual, I promised to call as soon as I arrived home safely.

A mag[83] problem and wx delays made the trip longer than normal, but I eventually got there and had this exchange:

Me: "Indianapolis Approach, N12345, landing Indianapolis with (current ATIS designation)."

Indy Approach: "N12345, is there a 'Mark' on board?"

Me, sheepishly: "Uhh, yes."

Indy Approach: *"Call Your Mother!"*

A flight dispatcher watches a plane landing tail-end forward. *"Flight 757, What The Hell Is Going On?"* He shouts into the microphone. *"Let Me Speak To The Captain!"*

"The c ..., the c ..., the captain is drunk."

"Then Give Me The Second Pilot!"

"H ..., he`s d ..., drunk too."

"Well, then, who`s talking?"

"The A ..., Autop ..., Autopilot ...."

Airline pilots, like any of us, can have a tough time finding their way around an unfamiliar airport. One day at SJC (San Jose, CA.), a UAL DC-10 was headed into unfamiliar territory.

---

83 Magneto

Controllers observed the aircraft come to a full stop just short of an intersecting taxiway and remain motionless.

After a moment, Ground Control called and said, "UAL 684, turn right at that taxiway."

There was no response.

Again the controller said, "UAL 684, turn right at that taxiway."

No response.

After a few seconds, the controller tried a different approach: "UAL 684, turn toward the co-pilot," at which point the aircraft made an immediate ninety-degree turn to the right.

Chief FA during briefing: "Folks, we have someone celebrating his 65th birthday today by taking his first flight." (a round of applause follows)

"So on your way off the plane at [destination], be sure and stop by the cockpit and wish Capt. Jones a Happy Birthday."

A wife reports that her husband, an airline pilot, often has difficulty locating items around the house. One day he asked where the salt was. Annoyed, the wife responded, "How on earth can you find Detroit at night in a blizzard, but you can't find the salt in your own kitchen?"

"Well, darling," he replied, "they don't move Detroit."

"I can see the country club down below. Looks like a lot of controllers out there!"

"Yes, sir, there is. They're caddying for DC-10 drivers like you."

On a small commuter flight one sunny day, the captain was told that his passengers were nervous about being on a "small airplane." He decided to take action. "Good afternoon ladies and gentlemen. This is your captain. I've been informed that some of you are nervous about being on a 'little' plane. Well, let me assure you, there's nothing to worry about. Just sit back and take it easy.

It might be helpful to do some sight-seeing to put your mind at ease. Now, if you'll all lean and look out over the right wing of the airplane, it'll tip over!

Hahahahaha! A little pilot humor there."

Several times a week I drive by the Aurora, IL airport with one or both of my twin daughters. On one night as we drove by fairly late, my daughter Jaime noticed that the runway lights were on.

"Dad," she said, "I thought you said the airport was closed at night."

I was surprised at her notice of that bit of trivia and answered, "Yes, that's right; it closed about an hour ago."

"Then why are the lights still on?" she queried.

I explained that the airport was equipped with pilot-controlled lighting, and that if the pilot clicks the mike button a few times in quick succession, the lights come on.

Jaime digested this information for a moment, then asked, "Is that like a 'Clapper' for old pilots?"

"Son, I've got more time sitting on the lav in this airliner than you have total time in the air." Also heard: "And I've got more time in the bunk." Or, "Son, your wife's legs have more time in the air than you do."

— Welcome to a new co-pilot from an old captain.

Son, I was flying airplanes for a living when you were still in liquid form.

This was at SBN (South Bend, IN). I was getting ready to depart IFR for Oshkosh in a Cessna Cardinal.

Me: "Oshkosh ground, Cessna 1546 Hotel at the ramp, taxi IFR Oshkosh."

Ground: "Cessna 46 Hotel is cleared to Oshkosh Airport via [insert complete IFR clearance here]."

It seems to vary from one airport to another when and how you pick up an IFR clearance. At my home base I'm used to saying "Taxi IFR" and getting a taxi clearance along with the advisory "clearance on request" (which means that the ground controller had already asked ATC for my clearance). In any event, it's quite a surprise to receive an entire IFR clearance in one gulp when you've asked only for a taxi clearance.

Fortunately, I was up to it. I had pencil and paper within easy reach and started copying frantically.

Me: "46 Hotel cleared to Oshkosh via [repeat entire clearance here]."

Ground: "Read back is correct. Twin Cessna 46 Hotel, taxi runway 029."

The ultimate compliment on radio technique! So I set out to taxi to the runway.

That's when I discovered I'd forgotten to untie the tail.

Standard checklist philosophy requires that pilots read to each other the actions they perform every flight and recite from memory those they need every three years.

Pilot: "Washington Radar, United 916, we've just been struck by tremendous lightning!"

Controller: "United 916, roger, do you have any problems?"

Pilot: "Not really. We just have to change our underwear."

A Mexican newspaper reports that bored Royal Air Force pilots stationed on the Falkland Islands have devised a marvelous new game.

Noting that the local penguins are fascinated by airplanes, the pilots search out a beach where the birds are gathered and fly slowly along at the water's edge. Perhaps ten thousand penguins turn their heads in unison watching the planes go by. When the pilots turn around and fly back, the birds turn their heads in the opposite direction, like spectators at a slow-motion tennis match.

Then, the paper reports, "The pilots fly out to sea and directly back to the penguin colony and over it. Heads go up, up, up, and ten thousand penguins fall over gently onto their backs."

A preacher dies and goes to heaven, where he's greeted at the gate by St. Peter. "Who are you?" St. Peter asks.

"I'm Joe Brown. I'm a preacher. I've been preaching the Word of God for fifty years!"

"Hmmm," St. Peter says, "Let me check and see if you can come inside."

Peter wanders off into Heaven. While he's gone, someone else comes to the gate and knocks. Peter promptly returns to the gate and asks the new arrival, "Who are you?" "I'm Stan Smith," the guy replies.

"Stan Smith? Stan Smith, the pilot? St. Peter exclaims."

"Why, that's right," the guy replies.

St. Peter throws open the gate and ushers the new arrival inside with an enthusiastic "Come in! Come in!"

"What about me?" asks Preacher Brown.

"Give it a few more minutes. We're still checking," St. Peter replies and shuts the gate again. After what seems like hours, St. Peter comes back to the gate and opens it. "We've checked, and it's been decided you can come in," he tells the preacher.

The preacher walks in. While St. Peter is escorting him to his eternal reward, he asks, "You know, I don't want to seem jealous or resentful, but I've been preaching the Word of God for fifty years, but it took you forever to decide if I could come in. But you practically pulled that pilot out of his shoes getting him inside Heaven's gate. What gives?"

"Well," Peter replies, "for fifty years while you preached, people slept in the pews. But every time someone got aboard an airplane with Stan, they were praying their hearts out!"

— Sue Critz

A British Airways mechanic passes away. Upon being met at the Pearly Gates, he is asked by St. Peter what is his most heartfelt desire. "To *never* be around any BA captains!" was his emphatic response. A few weeks later, while relaxing in the Angel's lounge, who should walk in but a British Airways captain in all his regalia. Furious, the mechanic marches off to find St. Peter to complain.

St. Peter calms the man by saying, "There are no BA captains in Heaven. That was God. He just likes to pretend that he is one."

— Frank Brandt

Three airline pilots arrived at the Golden Gate for their eternal assignments. The guide greeted them, and they got on an elevator. The first stop was at the top of heaven; great view, private bath, library, the works. Turning to the United pilot, he said, "Here you are," and left with the other two.

The elevator descended to a lower level, and the Trans World pilot was assigned to a typical motel room; bath, closet; comfortable, but nothing exceptional.

The guide then took the remaining pilot to the lower levels, where he was assigned to a sparse room; bunk, table, chair, clothes rack; nothing else.

The pilot, an American type, said, "I don't like to complain, at least I'm here, but why do I get such a plain place when the United bum got such a cozy suite?"

"Simple," said the guide, "We've never had anybody from United here before."

— Jerry Marlette

Little boy to airline pilot: "You're a pilot! That must be exciting!"

Pilot: "Not if I do it right."

On a small charter plane, immediately after liftoff, the pilot began to open his flight plan. A few seconds later, he turned to his passengers and inquired as to what time it was.

After getting the correct time and opening his plan, he tapped his watch and remarked that he was surprised that it had stopped, because he usually changed the batteries in it the same time that he changed the batteries in his pacemaker.

— Gary T. Craze, gcraze@bangate.compaq.com

Flight on ATR[84] 42 from Lyon to Rennes (France). As passengers were seated by the Hostess, that nice girl closed the door and walked to the cabin in order to inform the pilots. At that moment, I noticed two guys standing outside, arms crossed, looking at the airplane and smiling.

A few seconds later, the hostess raced down the aisle, red faced, explaining that she forgot the pilots outside!

— Francois, micro_tech@msn.com

There once was a captain who enjoyed pranks. As the legend goes, one day he found an unmarked white cane in the

---

84 Regional turboprop aircraft

terminal. Digging through his bag of goodies, he donned a set of extra-thick gag glasses and fumbled his way across the ramp to his parked aircraft.

The passengers watched as he groped his way up the airstairs and into the main entry. "Hi, Marsha," he sang out as he felt for the cockpit doorknob. Pausing, he looks back and forth over the heads of the startled passengers. Through the huge lens, his eyes are three times their normal size. "Say, Marsha, are we hauling freight or passengers today?"

The matronly attendant smiles graciously and replies softly, "Umm. Passengers, Sir."

Our hero raises his watch to within an inch to his glasses, and announces for all to hear, "Well, then, we'd better start getting them aboard! It's nearly time to leave!"

Heard while flying in Holland. Tower talking to a female helicopter pilot.

Tower: "What's your altitude?"

Pilot: "1000 feet."

Tower: "What's your heading?"

Pilot: "175."

Tower: "What's your speed?"

Pilot: "150 knots."

Tower: "What's your bra size?"

Pilot: "36B... *Aaawwwwww–Shhiiiiiittttt!*"

A friend of a friend, who is an airline co-pilot, told the following stories about a captain with whom he often flew. This guy was an excellent pilot, but not real good at making passengers feel at ease.

For example, one time the airplane in front of him blew a tire on landing, scattering chunks of rubber all over the runway. He was asked to hold while the trucks came out and cleaned up.

His announcement: "Ladies and gentlemen, I'm afraid there will be a short delay before our arrival. They've closed the airport while they clean up what's left of the last airplane that landed there."

Then there was the time they were flying through turbulence. Some of the passengers became alarmed at how much the wings were bending in the rough air. One of the flight attendants relayed that message to the captain.

His announcement: "Ladies and gentlemen, I've been informed that some of you have noticed our wings bending in the turbulence. In fact, the flight attendant told me that the wing tips are bending as much as ten feet in the bumps. Well, that's perfectly normal; there's nothing to worry about. Our wings are designed to bend as much as thirteen feet at the tips and, as you can see, we're nowhere near that yet."

I was on a night flight from a small western city. The take-off path was over a rural valley, darkened except for the lights that twinkled from occasional farm houses. Shortly after take-off, the plane's lights began flashing on and off. Then the pilot announced over the loudspeaker system: "In case you're wondering why I'm blinking the landing lights, look over to your left and you'll see a flashing light on the hillside. My youngsters are saying, 'Goodnight, Dad,' in Morse code. I'm just acknowledging the message."

After a brief pause, the plane's lights began flashing again. "It's past their bedtime," the pilot announced. "I just signaled them to go to bed." Sure enough, the lights on the hillside went out.

"Please don't tell Mum I'm a pilot. She thinks I play piano in a whorehouse."

What are the two most dangerous things in aviation? A doctor in a Bonanza and two Chief pilots in a DC-9.

Everything is accomplished through teamwork until something goes wrong. Then, one pilot gets all the blame.

"This is your Captain speaking. These stupid planes are a lot different than the ships I'm used to, so you'll have to give me some leeway."

THE CO-PILOT

I am the co-pilot. I sit on the right. It's up to me to be quick and bright; I never talk back if I have regrets, but I have to remember what the Captain forgets.

I make out the Flight Plan and study the weather, pull up the gear, stand by to feather[85], make out the mail forms, and do the reporting, and fly the old crate while the Captain is courting.

I take the readings, adjust the power, put on the heaters when we're in a shower, tell him where we are on the darkest night, and do all the bookwork without any light.

I call for my Captain and buy him Cokes. I always laugh at his corny jokes, and once in awhile when his landings are rusty I always come through with, "By gosh, it's gusty!"

All in all I'm a general stooge, as I sit on the right of the man I call "Scrooge". I guess you think that's past under-standing, but maybe someday he'll give me a landing.

— Keith Murray

---

85 Vary propeller pitch.

Don't forget the three things a good co-pilot knows how to say:

"Yes, sir"

"No, sir"

and "I'll take the ugly one, sir"

[for political correctness, substitute ma'am as required]

— cobbm (cobbm@usa.net)

The only soul more pitiful than a captain who cannot make up his mind is the co-pilot who has to fly with him.

PILOT RULES

The pilot always makes "The Rules."

"The Rules" are subject to change at any time without prior notification.

No co-pilot can possibly know all "The Rules."

If the pilot suspects the co-pilot knows all "The Rules," he must immediately change some or all of "The Rules."

The pilot is never wrong.

If the pilot is wrong, it is due to a misunderstanding which was a direct result of something the co-pilot did or said wrong. The co-pilot must apologize immediately for causing such misunderstanding.

The pilot may change his mind at any time. The co-pilot must never change his mind without the express written consent of the pilot.

The pilot has every right to be angry or upset at any time. The co-pilot must remain calm at all times unless the pilot wants him to be angry and/or upset.

The co-pilot is expected to mind read at all times.

The pilot is ready when he is ready.

The co-pilot must be ready at all times.

Any attempt to document "The Rules" could result in bodily harm.

The co-pilot who doesn't abide by "The Rules" is grounded.

— Wellemans Thierry

(UPI) LONG BEACH, Calif. Look, up in the sky. Is it a bird, a plane, the space shuttle? No, it's Larry Walters at 16,000 feet in his lawn chair.

Walters, 33, a truck driver, spent nearly two hours in the air on Friday in an aluminum lawn chair suspended from a fifty-foot cable attached to 45 helium-filled balloons.

Among other things, he threw a scare into a couple of air-line pilots who happened across the path of his weird flying contraption.

"I know it sounds strange, but it's true," said a Long Beach police officer. "The guy just filled up some balloons with helium, strapped on a parachute, grabbed a BB gun, and took off."

But everything didn't go as planned and Walters had a few dicey moments as he started getting numb in the cold atmosphere at 16,000 feet and decided to descend, which he accomplished by popping some of the balloons with the BB gun. As he neared the ground, he saw power lines.

"That's when I got scared," he said. "Those things can fry you."

He didn't get fried. The balloons draped themselves across the wires, leaving Walters dangling in his chair a few feet from the ground. Finally he dropped to earth. The landing knocked out power in the neighborhood for twenty minutes.

"I've fulfilled my twenty-year dream," said Walters, a truck driver for a company that makes TV commercials. "I'm staying on the ground. I've proved to myself that the thing works."

In addition to the BB gun and the parachute, Walter carried several one-gallon water jugs for ballast, a life vest and a CB radio.

"But the best piece of equipment was the lawn chair," Walters said. "It was a Sears. It was extremely comfortable."

Walters told authorities that he was trying to drift to the Mojave Desert, the site of Sunday's scheduled space shuttle Columbia landing, but the winds didn't cooperate.

"I wasn't trying to upstage the space shuttle," Walters said. "I would have landed well away from there. I just wanted to lay back and enjoy it all, but I had to do something when my toes started getting numb."

Police said they probably wouldn't file charges against Walters. But the Federal Aviation Administration was investigating, mainly because of the scare Walters gave the airline pilots who came across him at 16,000 feet in his flying lawn chair.

FOURTEEN

Pilot Quotes

"More than anything else, the sensation is one of perfect peace mingled with an excitement that strains every nerve to the utmost, if you can conceive of such a combination."

— Wilbur Wright

"The exhilaration of flying is too keen, the pleasure too great, for it to be neglected as a sport."

— Orville Wright

"The most beautiful dream that has haunted the heart of man since Icarus is today reality."

— Louis Bleriot

"You haven't seen a tree until you've seen its shadow from the sky."

— Amelia Earhart

"By day, or on a cloudless night, a pilot may drink the wine of the gods, but it has an earthly taste. He's a god of the earth, like one of the Grecian deities who lives on worldly mountains and descended for intercourse with men. But at night, over a stratus layer, all sense of the planet may disappear. You know that, down below, beneath that heavenly blanket is the earth, factual and hard.

But it's an intellectual knowledge, a knowledge tucked away in the mind, not a feeling that penetrates the body. And if at times you renounce experience and mind's heavy logic, it seems that the world has rushed along on its orbit, leaving you alone flying above a forgotten cloud bank, somewhere in the solitude of interstellar space."
— Charles A. Lindbergh, *The Spirit of St. Louis*

"I decided that if I could fly for ten years before I was killed in a crash, it would be a worthwhile trade for an ordinary lifetime."
— Charles A. Lindbergh, *The Spirit of St. Louis*

If God had meant for men to fly, He would have made their bones hollow and not their heads.

If God meant man to fly, he'd have given him more money.

Why did God invent women when airplanes were so much fun?

"If God had meant Icarus to fly, He would have given him a cloudy day."
— Leon M. Wise

"They say it's better than sex. It's so much better. It's amazing."
— Angelina Jolie, pilot and actress, regards flying,reported in *In Touch Weekly*, 4 July 2005.

"Flying is like sex. I've never had all I wanted, but occasionally I've had all I could stand."
— Stephen Coonts, *The Cannibal Queen*

"If God had intended man to fly, He would not have invented Spanish Air Traffic Control."

> — Lister, in the BBC
> TV series, *Red Dwarf*

As a pilot, only two bad things can happen to you. One of them will be:

- One day you'll walk out to the aircraft knowing that it's your last flight.
- One day you'll walk out to the airplane not knowing that it's your last flight.

One of the beautiful things about a single-piloted aircraft is the quality of the social experience.

The propeller is just a big fan in front of the plane used to keep the pilot cool. Don't believe it? Watch the pilot start sweating if it stops.

The only time you have too much fuel is when you're on fire.

In the aviation business, you can't get something for nothing. But if you aren't careful, you'll get nothing for something.

A pilot lives in a world of perfection, or not at all.

> — Richard S. Drury

When you're sitting in the rubber raft looking up where your airplane used to be, it's too late to re-check the flight plan.

"A pilot who doesn't have any fear, probably isn't flying his plane to its maximum."

> — Jon McBride, astronaut

A smooth landing is mostly luck. Two in a row is all luck. Three in a row is a prevarication.

A thunderstorm is nature's way of saying, "Up yours, sucker!"

"Always keep an 'out' in your hip pocket."
— Bevo Howard

Always try to keep the number of landings you make equal to the number of takeoffs.

"An airplane might disappoint any pilot, but it'll never surprise a good one."
— Len Morgan

"Death is just nature's way of telling you to watch your airspeed."
— Anon

The last thing every pilot does before leaving the aircraft after making a gear up landing is to put the gear selection lever in the *down* position.

Any flight over water in a single engine airplane will absolutely guarantee abnormal engine noises and vibrations.

Don't drop the aircraft to fly the microphone. An aeroplane flies because of a principle discovered by Bernoulli, not Marconi. Stated in a different fashion, "unskilled" pilots are always found in the wreckage with their hand wrapped around the microphone.

Flying the airplane is more important than radioing your plight to a person on the ground incapable of understanding or doing anything about it.

"Don't ever let an airplane take you someplace where your brain hasn't arrived at least a couple of minutes earlier."
— Andy Anderson

Flashlights are tubular metal containers kept in a flight bag for the purpose of storing dead batteries.

Fly it until the last piece stops moving.

"Flying an aeroplane with only a single propeller to keep you in the air. Can you imagine that?"
— Captain Picard, from *Star Trek: The Next Generation* episode "*Booby Trap*"

Flying is hours of boredom, punctuated by moments of stark terror.

Try not to die all tensed up.

Gravity always wins!

"I hate to wake up and find my co-pilot asleep."
— Michael Treacy

"I hope you either take up parachute jumping or stay out of single-motored airplanes at night."
— Charles Lindbergh to Wiley Post, 1931

I remember when sex was safe and flying was dangerous.

I'd rather be a chicken than a turkey.

If all you can see out of the window is ground that's going round and round and all you can hear is commotion coming from the passenger compartment, things are not at all as they should be.

"If an airplane is still in one piece, don't cheat on it; ride the bastard down."

> — Ernest K. Gann, author & aviator

"If it has wheels, propellers or tits, sooner or later, it's bound to give you trouble."

> — Phyllis Moses, phylmoses@msn.com

If we are what we eat, then some pilots should eat more chicken.

"If you can't afford to do something right, then be darn sure you can afford to do it wrong."

> — Charlie Nelson

If you push the stick forward, the houses get bigger; if you pull the stick back, they get smaller. (Unless you keep pulling the stick back, then they get bigger again.)

You can only tie the record for flying low.

Seen on an aircraft insurance claim: "Description of loss: Hard landing caused by altitude change."

Clocks lie. An eighteen-hour layover passes much quicker that an eight-hour day.

Jet airplanes are just an expensive way of changing JP-4 into noise.

"There are old pilots, and there are bold pilots, but there are no old, bold pilots."

— W. W. Windstaff

Assumption is the mother of all f**k-ups.

When a flight is proceeding incredibly well, something was forgotten.

Just remember, if you crash because of weather, your funeral will be held on a sunny day.

It's better to die than to look bad, but it's possible to do both.

Death is a small price to pay for looking shit hot.

About aerobatics: It's like having sex and being in a car wreck at the same time.

"If you want to grow old as a pilot, you've got to know when to push it and when to back off."

— Chuck Yeager

"If you're faced with a forced landing, fly the thing as far into the crash as possible."

— Bob Hoover (renowned aerobatic and test pilot)

IFR = I Follow Roads.

"In the Alaska bush, I'd rather have a two hour bladder and three hours of gas than vice versa."

— Kurt Wien

"It occurred to me that if I did not handle the crash correctly, there would be no survivors."

— Richard Leakey, after engine failure in a single-engine aircraft. Nairobi, Kenya, 1993

It's better to be down here wishing you were up there, instead of up there wishing you were down here.

It's easy to make a small fortune in aviation. Step number one: Start with a large fortune.

Keep looking around. There's always something you've missed.

"Keep thy airspeed up, less the earth come from below and smite thee."

— William Kershner

Learn from the mistakes of others. You won't live long enough to make all of them yourself.

Never trade luck for skill.

"Real confidence in the air is bred only by mistakes made and recovered from at a safe altitude, in a safe ship, seated on a good parachute."

— Rodney H. Jackson

Regarding engine power: Lots is good, more is better, and too much is just enough.

Reliable sources also report that mountains have been known to hide out in clouds.

Remember, gravity is not just a good idea, it's the law. It's not subject to repeal.

Speed is life. Altitude is life insurance. No one has ever collided with the sky.

Stay out of clouds. The silver lining everyone keeps talking about might be another airplane going in the opposite direction.

Takeoffs are optional. Landings are mandatory.

"The Boeing 747 is so big that it's been said that it doesn't fly; the earth merely drops out from under it."
— Capt. Ned Wilson, Pan Am

"The emergencies you train for almost never happen. It's the one you can't train for that kills you."
— Ernest K. Gann, advice from the 'Old Pelican'

"The light at the end of the tunnel is another airplane's landing light coming down head-on to the runway you're taking off from."
— Robert Livingston, *Flying The Aeronca*

The only thing worse than a captain who never flew as co-pilot is a co-pilot who once was a captain.

The three most common phrases in airline aviation are "Was that for us?", "What'd he say?", and "Oh Shit!"

Since computers are now involved in flying, a new one has been added: "What's it doing now?"

The medical profession is the natural enemy of the aviation profession.

Ever notice that the only experts who decree that the age of the pilot is over are people who have never flown anything? Also, in spite of the intensity of their feelings that the pilot's day is over, I know of no such expert who has volunteered to be a passenger in a non-piloted aircraft.

He who demands everything that his aircraft can give him is a pilot. He who demands one iota more is a fool.

The worst day of flying still beats the best day of real work.

ABOUT NIGHT FLYING:

Remember that the airplane doesn't know that it's dark.

On a clear, moonless night, never fly between the tanker's lights.

There are certain aircraft sounds that can only be heard at night.

If you're going to night fly, it might as well be in weather (bad) so you can double your exposure to both hazards.

You would have to pay a lot of money at a lot of amusement parks and perhaps add a few drugs to get the same blend of psychedelic sensations as a single-engine night weather flight.

One of the most important skills that a pilot must develop is the skill to ignore those things that were designed by non-pilots to get the pilot's attention.

At the end of the day, the controllers, ops supervisors, maintenance guys, weather guessers, and birds are all trying to kill you. Your job is not to let them.

Remember that the radio is only an electronic suggestion box for the pilot. Sometimes the only way to clear up a problem is to turn it off.

What's the similarity between air traffic controllers and pilots?
If the pilot screws up, the pilot dies. If ATC screws up, the pilot dies.

When in doubt, hold on to your altitude. No one has ever collided with the sky.

To most people, the sky is the limit. To those who love aviation, the sky is home.

When one engine fails on a twin-engine airplane, you always have enough power left to get you to the scene of the crash.

When starting an aviation career, it's not unusual to be overwhelmed, terrified, suffer from lack of confidence, and be just plain scared. As experience grows, self-confidence replaces fear. But after a time, when you think you've seen it all, you realize your initial reactions were correct.

A check ride ought to be like a skirt, short enough to be interesting, but still be long enough to cover everything.

A good simulator check ride is like successful surgery on a corpse.

A thunderstorm is never as bad on the inside as it appears on the outside. It's worse!

The future in aviation is the next thirty seconds. Long-term planning is an hour and a half.

Airspeed, altitude, and brains. Two are always needed to successfully complete the flight.

Any attempt to stretch fuel is guaranteed to increase headwind.

Any comment about how well things are going is an absolute guarantee of trouble.

Any pilot who relies on a terminal[86] forecast can be sold Niagara Falls.

Aviation is not so much a profession as it is a disease.

Good judgment comes from experience. Unfortunately, the experience usually comes from poor judgment.

In the ongoing battle between objects made out of aluminum going hundreds of miles per hour and the ground going zero miles per hour, the ground has yet to lose.

---

86 Made near airport

Mankind has a perfect record in aviation. We've never left one up there!

Pilots believe in clean living. They never drink whiskey from a dirty glass.

The nicer an aeroplane looks, the better it flies.

Work hard, fly hard, play hard, and stay hard.

The probability of survival is inversely proportional to the angle of arrival. The larger the angle of arrival, the smaller the probability of survival, and vice versa.

Things which do you no good in aviation:
> Altitude above you.
> Runways behind you.
> Fuel in the truck.
> Half a second ago.
> The airspeed you don't have.

Those who hoot with the owls by night shouldn't fly with the eagles by day.

Three things kill young pilots in Alaska: weather, weather, and weather.

Try to keep the number of your landings equal to the number of your takeoffs.

Try to stay in the middle of the air. Don't go near the edges of it. The edges of the air can be recognized by the appearance of ground, buildings, sea, trees and interstellar space. It's much more difficult to fly there.

Weather forecasts are horoscopes with numbers.

GREATEST LIES IN AVIATION

Me? I've never busted minimums[87].

We'll be on time, maybe even early.

I have no interest in flying for the airlines.

All that turbulence spoiled my landing.

I'm a member of the Mile High Club[88].

I only need glasses for reading.

I broke out right at minimums.

The weather is gonna be all right. It's clearing to VFR.

Don't worry about the weight and balance. It'll fly.

If we get a little lower, I think we'll see the lights.

I'm 22, got 6000 hours, a four year degree, and 3000 hours in a Lear.

I'd love to have a woman co-pilot.

All you have to do is follow the book.

This plane outperforms the book by twenty percent.

We in aviation are overpaid, under-worked, and well respected.

Oh sure, no problem. I've got over 2000 hours in that aircraft.

No need to look that up, I've got it all memorized.

Sure, I can fly it. It has wings, doesn't it?

We'll be home by lunchtime.

I'm always glad to see the FAA.

We fly every day. We don't need recurrent training.

---

87 Minimum conditions for flying
88 Sexual intercourse above 5,280 feet

It just came out of annual[89]. How could anything be wrong?

I thought *you* took care of that.

I've got the field in sight.

I've got the traffic[90] in sight.

Of course, I know where we are.

I'm *sure* the gear was down.

---

89 Yearly service
90 Other aircraft.

FIFTEEN

Flying

"The natural function of the wing is to soar upwards and carry that which is heavy up to the place where dwells the race of gods. More than any other thing that pertains to the body, it partakes of the nature of the divine."

— Plato, *Phaedrus*

"Man must rise above the Earth, to the top of the atmosphere and beyond, for only thus will he fully understand the world in which he lives."

— Socrates

"The great bird will take its first flight filling the world with amazement and all records with its fame, and it will bring eternal glory to the nest where it was born."

— Leonardo da Vinci

"My soul is in the sky."

— William Shakespeare, A *Midsummer Night's Dream* Act V. Scene 1

"I'm getting housemaid's knee kneeling here gulping beauty."

— Amelia Earhart, comment in logbook, 1928

"He did it alone. We had a cast of a million."

— Neil Armstrong, regarding Charles Lindbergh

"I live for that exhilarating moment when I'm in an airplane rushing down the runway and pull on the stick and feel lift under its wings. It's a magical feeling to climb toward the heavens, seeing objects and people on the ground grow smaller and more insignificant. You have left that world beneath you. You are inside the sky."

— Gordon 'Gordo' Cooper, *Leap of Faith*

"If you have flown, perhaps you can understand the love a pilot develops for flight. It is much the same emotion a man feels for a woman, or a wife for her husband."

— Louise Thaden, co-founder of the *Ninety-Nines*

"Flying is an act of conquest, of defeating the most basic and powerful forces of nature. It unites the violent rage and brute power of jet engines with the infinitesimal tolerances of the cockpit. Airlines take their measurements from the ton to the milligram, from the mile to the millimeter, endowing any careless move: an engine setting, a flap position, a training failure - with the power to wipe out hundreds of lives."

— Thomas Petzinger, Jr. First couple of sentences of the prologue to *Hard Landing*

"You can always tell when a man has lost his soul to flying. The poor bastard is hopelessly committed to stopping whatever he's doing long enough to look up and make sure the aircraft purring overhead continues on course and does not suddenly fall out of the sky. It is also his bound duty to watch every aircraft within view take off and land."

— Ernest K Gann, *Fate Is The Hunter*

"Buddy of mine once told me that he'd rather fly a jet than kiss his girl. Said it gave him more of a kick."

— Jerry Connell, in the movie *Air Cadet*

"Any pilot can describe the mechanics of flying. What it can do for the spirit of man is beyond description."

— Barry M. Goldwater, US Senator

These beguiling ideas about science quoted here were supposedly gleaned from essays, exams, and classroom discussions. Most were from fifth and sixth graders. Some seem to apply to the art of flight.

The law of gravity says no fair jumping up without coming back down.

Clouds are high-flying fogs.

I'm not sure how clouds get formed. But the clouds know how to do it, and that's the important thing.

Water vapor gets together in a cloud. When it's big enough to be called a drop, it does.

Humidity is the experience of looking for air and finding water.

Rain is often known as soft water, oppositely known as hail.

Rain is saved up in cloud banks.

A blizzard is when it snows sideways.

Isotherms and isobars are even more important than their names sound.

Rainbows are just to look at, not to really understand.

A hurricane is a breeze of a bigly size.

YOU KNOW YOU'RE TRAVELING TOO MUCH WHEN:

You see the same flight attendant twice in the same day on different flights. And she knows your name.

You go to the movie theater, sit down and reach for the seat belts.

You see airport codes on car license plates (i.e. BNA — Nashville, MCO — Orlando…).

You hear a syndicated radio show in New York, fly west and listen to the same show hours later because its tape delayed.

Your frequent flyer statement is two pages long.

You call the restaurant waitress, "flight attendant."

You don't mind riding coach to Europe because it's a short flight.

You rent three cars on the same day in different cities.

All of your pens and notepads at home have different hotel names on them.

Good morning. As we leave Dallas, it's warm, the sun is shining, and the birds are singing. We're going to Charlotte, where it's dark, windy and raining. Why in the world y'all wanna go there, I really don't know.

Q: Why did Santa Claus ask Rudolph to lead his sleigh team?

A: Rudolph was the only one who was IFR current.

There was an airplane full of a Pepsi shipment flying somewhere over Africa. It suddenly had a malfunction and went down somewhere. A few weeks later, PepsiCo sent a rescue plane out to look for the lost aircraft. They found the wreckage, but were unable to locate the crew. They searched the area and found a tribe of cannibals.

They walked up to the Chief of the tribe and asked if he knew anything about the crash. The Chief goes, "Yeah." When asked where the crew was, the Chief replied, "We ate the crew, and we drank the Pepsi."

The rescue crew was shocked. One man asked, "Did you eat their legs?"

The chief replied, "We ate their legs, and we drank the Pepsi."

Another rescuer asked, "Did you eat their arms?"

The Chief said, "We ate their arms, and we drank the Pepsi."

After looking totally perplexed for a minute, a third asked, "Did you, you know... eat their... things??"

The chief says, "No."

"No?" asked the rescuers.

"No," replied the Chief. *Things* go better with Coke."

A search and rescue team had been assembled and sent on a mission to find an airplane that had crashed on top of a mountain. It was their duty to rescue survivors.

After finally reaching the top of the mountain, they came upon the crash site. At the site, one lone survivor sat with his back against a tree, chewing on a bone. As he tossed the bone onto a huge pile of bones, he noticed the rescue team. "Thank God," he cried out in relief. "I'm saved!"

The rescue team didn't move, as they were in shock, seeing the pile of human bones beside this lone survivor. Obviously he had eaten his comrades.

The survivor saw the horror in their faces and hung his head in shame. "You can't judge me for this," he insisted. "I had to survive. Is it so wrong to want to live?"

The leader of the rescue team stepped forward, shaking his head in disbelief. "I won't judge you for doing what was necessary to survive, but, my God man, your plane only went down yesterday!"

An airliner was suffering through a severe thunderstorm. As the passengers were being bounced around by the turbulence, a young woman turned to a priest sitting next to her and, with a nervous laugh, asked, "Father, you're a man of God. Can't you do something about this storm?"

To which he replied, "Lady, I'm in sales, not management."

You're flying in a small, single engine plane. You look up and see a hurricane directly ahead. What's the first thing that enters your mind?

This is the last time I fly no-frills.

I can't believe she's going to get *Everything* now!

I gotta change my shorts!

The windshield.

It only takes two things to fly: airspeed and money.

It's best to keep the pointed end going forward as much as possible.

Life is simple. Eat, sleep, fly.

"Never fly anything that doesn't have the paint worn off the rudder pedals."

— Harry Bill

Never fly in the same cockpit with someone braver than you.

"Never fly the 'A' model of anything."

— Ed Thompson

In the space age, man will be able to go around the world in two hours. One hour for flying and one hour to get to the airport.

— Neil McElroy, *Look*, 1958.

Traveler's Toast: May you get a first class upgrade and an empty seat beside you.

Definition of jet lag: "Finding your wallet in the refrigerator and not remembering what you did with the milk."

A man in a hot air balloon realized he was lost.

He reduced altitude and spotted a woman below. He descended a bit more and shouted, "Excuse me, can you help me? I promised a friend I'd meet him an hour ago, but I don't know where I am."

The woman below replied, "You're in a hot air balloon hovering approximately thirty feet above the ground. You're between 40 and 41 degrees north latitude and between 59 and 60 degrees west longitude."

"You must be an engineer," said the balloonist.

"I am," replied the woman, "How did you know?"

"Well," answered the balloonist, "everything you told me is technically correct, but I have no idea what to make of your information and the fact is, I'm still lost. Frankly, you've not been much help so far."

The woman below responded, "You must be in Management."

"I am," replied the balloonist, "but how did you know?"

"Well," said the woman, "you don't know where you are or where you're going. You've risen to where you are due to a large quantity of hot air. You made a promise that you have no idea how to keep, and you expect people beneath you to solve your problems. The fact is, you're in exactly the same position you were in before we met, but now, somehow, it's my fault!"

Modern air travel would be enjoyable if I could only learn to enjoy boredom, discomfort, and fatigue.

Fred and his wife Edna went to the State Fair every year. Every year Fred would say, "Edna, I'd like to ride in that there airplane."

And every year Edna would say, "I know Fred, but that airplane ride costs ten dollars, and ten dollars is ten dollars."

One year Fred and Edna went to the Fair and Fred said, "Edna, I'm 71 years old. If I don't ride that airplane this year, I may never get another chance."

Edna replied, "Fred, that there airplane ride costs ten dollars, and ten dollars is ten dollars."

The pilot overheard them and said, "Folks, I'll make you a deal. I'll take you both up for a ride. If you can stay quiet for the entire ride and not say one word, I won't charge you, but if you say one word, it's ten dollars."

Fred and Edna agreed and up they go. The pilot does all kinds of twists and turns, rolls and dives, but not a word is heard. He does all his tricks over again, but still not a word. They land and the pilot turns to Fred. "By golly, I did everything I could think of to get you to yell out, but you didn't."

Fred replied, "Well, I was gonna say something when Edna fell out, but ten dollars is ten dollars."

Two hunters hired a bush pilot to fly them to a remote lake in Alaska. As he dropped them off, the pilot said, "Now, you can legally shoot one moose apiece, but don't do it. We can't possibly get out of here with two moose strapped onto the pontoons." The hunters promised, but temptation was too great. They shot two.

When the pilot returned to pick them up, he screamed and hollered, but finally they strapped a moose to each pontoon. Went to the downwind end of the lake, firewalled[91] it, finally lifted off just before the far shore. The plane struggled to climb, but the terrain rose faster. They went into the trees.

When the noise quieted down, the pilot said, "I told you SOBs we couldn't get out of this lake with two moose aboard!"

One hunter replied, "Well, we got about a half mile farther than we did last year!"

— vince norris, penn state u.

An Englishman, Frenchman, Mexican, and Texan were flying across country in a small plane when the pilot comes on the loud speaker and says, "We're having mechanical problems. The only way we can make it to the next airport is for three of you to open the door and jump. You'll have to determine who."

The four open the door and look out below. The Englishman takes a deep breath and hollers, "God save the Queen" and jumps. The Frenchman gets really inspired and hollers, "Viva La France" and he also jumps.

This really pumps up the Texan, so he hollers, "Remember the Alamo," grabs the Mexican and throws him out of the plane.

Three passengers board a small airplane; the President, the Pope and a hippie. Later, the pilot tells them the plane is in trouble. There are only two parachutes for them, so they have to figure out who will be left without one. The President

---

91 Same as "pedal-to-the-metal."

immediately grabs a parachute and bolts out the door scream-ing, "I'm too important of a man to die!"

The Pope and the hippie look at the one remaining para-chute, then at each other. The Pope speaks. "My son, I've lived a good, long life, and I have faith that I will go to a better place. You take the last parachute, my son."

The hippie giggles and hands the Pope the parachute, say-ing "Nah, that's okay. You take this one. I'll take the other one. The President just jumped out with my knapsack."

On a transatlantic flight, a plane passes through a severe storm. The turbulence is awful, and things go from bad to worse when one wing is struck by lightning.

One woman in particular, loses it.

Screaming, she stands up in front of the plane. "I'm too young to die!" she wails. "Well, if I'm going to die, I want my last minutes of life to be memorable! Is there *anyone* on this plane who can make me feel like a *woman*?"

Then, a man stands up in the rear of the plane.

"I can make you feel like a woman," he says.

He's gorgeous. Tall, well-built with long, flowing black hair and bright, blue eyes. He starts to walk slowly up the aisle, unbuttoning his shirt one button at a time. No one moves.

The woman is breathing heavily in anticipation as the stranger approaches.

He removes his shirt. Muscles ripple across his chest as he reaches her and extends the arm holding his shirt to the trem-bling woman.

He demands, "Iron this."

A Delta Airlines jet was traversing Arizona on a clear day. The co-pilot was bombarding passengers with remarks about landmarks over the PA system.

"Coming up on the right side of our cabin, you can see Meteor Crater. A major tourist attraction in northern Arizona, it was formed when a lump of nickel and iron weighing 300,000 tons, 150 feet across, struck the earth at 40,000 miles an hour, scattering white-hot debris for miles in every direction. The hole measures nearly a mile across and is 570 feet deep."

From the cabin, a passenger was heard to exclaim, "Wow! It just missed the highway!"

One day at a busy airport, the passengers on a commercial airliner are seated, waiting for the cockpit crew to show up so they can get underway. The pilot and the co-pilot finally appear and begin walking up the center aisle to the cockpit. Both appear to be blind. The pilot is using a white cane, bumping into passengers left and right as he stumbles down the aisle. The co-pilot is using a guide dog. Both have their eyes covered with huge sun glasses.

At first, the passengers don't react, thinking that it must be some sort of joke. However, after a few minutes the engines start revving up, and the airplane starts moving down the runway. The passengers look at each other with some uneasiness, whispering among themselves and looking desperately to the flight attendants for reassurance.

Then the airplane starts accelerating rapidly and people begin to panic. Some passengers are praying. As the plane gets closer and closer to the end of the runway, the voices are becoming more and more hysterical. Finally, when the airplane has less than twenty feet of runway left, there's a sudden change in the pitch of the shouts as everyone screams at once, and at the very last moment the airplane lifts off and is airborne.

Up in the cockpit, the co-pilot breathes a sigh of relief and turns to the captain. "You know, one of these days the passengers aren't going to scream, and we're gonna get killed!"

On an airplane flight, I was skimming through a colorful safety information card written in French, Spanish, and English. I pointed out to my dozing husband that the French need just one word, *amerrissage,* to say, *landing on water.* "In English you can't express the thought *landing on water* with just one word," I said.

"Splash!" he murmured sleepily.

"Our loss of altitude allows a unique close-up perspective of the local terrain. I assure you that it's all part of our airlines new commitment to make your a flight a sight-seeing extravaganza."

"I'm sure everyone noticed the loss of an engine; however, the reduction in weight and drag will mean we'll be flying much more efficiently now."

"There are two kinds of airplanes, those you fly and those that fly you."

— Ernest K. Gann

"When asked by someone how much money flying takes: Why, all of it!"

— Gordon Baxter

"Get the parachutes ready."

A two-seater Cessna 152 plane crashed into a cemetery early this afternoon in central Poland. Polish search and rescue workers have recovered 300 bodies so far. They expect that number will climb as digging continues into the evening.

A woman on her first plane trip found herself a nice window seat in a no-smoking area. But no sooner had she settled down than a man appeared and insisted that it was his seat. Despite a lengthy argument, she flatly refused to move and told him to go away.

"Okay, madam," he said, "If that's the way you want it, you fly the plane."

"Ladies and gentlemen, Mabuhay! This is your Captain Biglangawa speaking. We are now over the Philippine trench where you can find the deepest part of the Pacific Ocean. Here you can also find almost all the ferocious creatures in the sea. There are the killer sharks, barracudas and many others.

Please, stay calm and don't panic. Both our engines are dead. We are now going down into that ocean. Please wear your life vest. We are going to crash land this plane into the water. In the meantime, I would like you to follow everything I'm going to say. Repeat after me:

Our Father who art in Heaven."

If it flies, floats, or f**ks, it's always cheaper to rent than to buy.

Always remember, you fly an aeroplane with your head, not your hands.

Flying is better than running. Running is better than walking. Walking is better than crawling. All of these, however, are better than an extraction by a Med-Evac helicopter, even if that is technically a form of flying.

Flying isn't dangerous. Crashing is dangerous.

Flying isn't Nintendo. You don't push a button and start over.

Flying is the perfect vocation for a man who wants to feel like a boy, but not for one who still is.

The NTSB[92] has determined that a frayed wire caused the spark that ignited vapors in the TWA flight 800 fuel tank. The wire became frayed when it was hit by a missile.

LONDON — A British couple who made love in a light aircraft forgot to turn off their transmitter. They broadcast their moments of passion to air traffic controllers, aircraft and radio enthusiasts on Wednesday.

The couple, flying in a private Cessna 150 plane near the Scottish City of Edinburgh, began by debating whether they should have sex 5,000 feet above ground and join the Mile High Club. Their conversation grew more and more passionate, then ceased, but the mike was still hot.

Fifteen aircraft, including shuttles, passenger jets and cargo planes, had to use an emergency channel while the two cavorted.

"We've been trying to raise you for the past fifty minutes," an angry controller was quoted by the domestic Press Association telling the couple when they came in to land.

"We've been listening to your conversation. Very interesting. Please come and see me after you park."

The pilot reported to authorities at Edinburgh Airport, where he was reprimanded for blocking radio communication, the Press Association reported.

---

92 National Transportation Safety Board

"Apart from one aspect of his airmanship, his failure to check in on a regular basis, there were no breaches of aviation rules," it quoted the airport's air traffic control manager Paul Louden as saying.

This story is true: told by the pilot and confirmed by ATC.

Southend ATC: "X Air 676, cleared for takeoff; report passing 2000 feet."

X Air 676: "Cleared for takeoff; call you passing 2000."

X Air 676: "Southend, 676 is climbing, passing 2000."

Southend ATC: "Call London 128.6 (change radio frequencies)."

X Air 676: "London 128.6, see you on the way home." (in the process of changing frequencies, 676 loses the door. Yes, the *door* on a BE 90)

X Air 676: "Mayday, Mayday, Mayday."

"London Control, this is X Air 676, four miles west of Southend, 2500 feet. I've lost the door. Climbing to 4000 feet and returning to Southend."

London ATC: "X Air 676, roger. Are you in control of the Aircraft?"

X Air 676: "No more than usual!"

Just turned off the ten o'clock channel Nine News in LA.

A single engine plane (identified as an Aero Commander) went down short of Burbank airport. Both people on board survived.

The pilot was lucid as he was being cut out of the wreckage. He said he ran out of fuel over Eagle Rock and was trying to make Burbank Airport.

Remarking about the lack of fire, the Fire Marshall in charge of the rescue said, "They're just lucky there was no fuel on board."

I was flying from San Francisco to Los Angeles. By the time we took off, there had been a 45-minute delay. Everybody on board was ticked. Unexpectedly, we stopped in Sacramento on the way. The flight attendant explained that there would be another 45-minute delay. If we wanted to get off the aircraft, we would re-board in thirty minutes.

Everybody got off the plane except one gentleman who was blind. I noticed him as I walked by. I could tell he had flown before because his Seeing Eye dog was laying quietly underneath the seats in front of him throughout the entire flight. I could also tell he had flown this very flight before because the pilot approached him and, calling him by name, said, "Keith, we're in Sacramento for almost an hour. Would you like to get off and stretch your legs?"

Keith replied, "No thanks, but maybe my dog would like to stretch his legs."

Picture this. All the people in the gate area came to a complete, quiet standstill when they looked up and saw the pilot walk off the plane with the Seeing Eye dog! The pilot was even wearing sunglasses.

People scattered. They not only tried to change planes, they also were trying to change airlines.

Flight seven-oh-niner has a pretty rough time above the ocean. Suddenly a voice comes over the intercom: "Ladies and gentlemen, please fasten your seat belts and assume crash positions. We've lost our engines and are trying to put this baby down as gently as possible on the water."

"Oh, flight attendant! Are there any sharks in the ocean below?" asks a little old lady, terrified.

"Yes, I'm afraid there are some. But not to worry, we have a special gel in the bottle next to your seat designed especially for emergencies like this. Just rub the gel on your arms and legs."

"And if I do this, the sharks won't eat me anymore?" asks the little old lady.

"Oh, they'll eat you, all right, only they won't enjoy it so much."

Your seat cushions can be used for floatation. In the event of an emergency water landing, please paddle to shore and take them with our compliments.

While cruising at 40,000 feet, the airplane shuddered, and Mr. Benson looked out the window.

"Good lord!" he screamed. "One of the engines just blew up!"

Other passengers left their seats and came rushing over. Suddenly, the aircraft was rocked by a second blast as yet another engine exploded on the other side.

The passengers were in a panic now. Even the flight attendants couldn't maintain order. Just then, standing tall and smiling confidently, the pilot strode from the cockpit and assured everyone that there was nothing to worry about. His words and his demeanor made most of the passengers feel better. They sat down as the pilot calmly walked to the door of the aircraft. There, he grabbed several packages from under the seats and began handing them to the flight attendants.

Each crew member attached the package to their backs. "Say," spoke up an alert passenger, "aren't those parachutes?"

The pilot said they were. The passenger went on, "But I thought you said there was nothing to worry about."

"There isn't," replied the pilot as a third engine exploded. "We're going to get help."

Changes at NASA to accommodate 76-Year-Old John Glenn's return to space aboard the Shuttle Discovery:

All important devices now operated by the Clapper.

Shuttle's thermostat set at eighty degrees.

Shuffleboard installed in cargo bay.

"Early Bird" specials from Morrison's Cafeteria included on menu.

One monitor specifically designated for *Matlock*.

Little bowls of candy scattered randomly about the ship.

Top speed of shuttle set at 25 miles per hour.

Installed a new bifocal windshield.

Space pants now go up to the armpits.

Left-blinker left on for entire mission.

Parachutists are good to the last drop. (found on a bumper sticker from a parachute school)

THE PARACHUTE PARADIGM

You're one of the people on a malfunctioning airplane with too few parachutes:

Pessimist: You refuse a parachute because you would die in the jump anyway.

Optimist: You refuse a parachute because people have survived jumps just like this before.

Procrastinator: You play a game of Monopoly for a parachute.

Engineer: You make another parachute out of aisle curtains and dental floss.

Surgeon General: You explain that skydiving can be hazardous to your health.

National Rifle Association member: You shoot another passenger and take a parachute.

Sports Fan: You start betting on how long it will take to crash.

Auto Mechanic: As long as you're looking at the engine, it works fine so a chute is unnecessary.

— Darrin McGraw

SIXTEEN

Military Air

"Another popular fallacy is to suppose that flying machines could be used to drop dynamite on an enemy in time of war."
— William H. Pickering, *Aeronautics*, 1908

"To affirm that the aeroplane is going to 'revolutionize' naval warfare of the future is to be guilty of the wildest exaggeration."
— *Scientific American*, 16 July 1910

"Airplanes are interesting toys, but of no military value."
— Marshal Ferdinand Foch,
Supreme Commander of Allied forces, 1918

"Aviation is good for sport, but for the Army it is useless!"
— Marshal Ferdinand Foch

"To throw bombs from an airplane will do as much damage as throwing bags of flour. It will be my pleasure to stand on the bridge of any ship while it is attacked by airplanes."
— Newton Baker, U.S. Minister of War (1921)

"For good or for ill, air mastery is today the supreme expression of military power. Fleets and armies, however vital and important, must accept a subordinate rank."

— Prime Minister Winston Churchill

"If we maintain our faith in God, love of freedom, and superior global air power, the future [of the US] looks good."

— General Curtis Lemay

DEPARTMENT OF THE ARMY.

Regulations For Operation Of Aircraft. Commencing January 1920.

Don't take the machine into the air unless you are satisfied it will fly.

Never leave the ground with the motor leaking.

Don't turn sharply when taxiing. Instead of turning sharp, have someone lift the tail around.

Never get out of the machine with the motor running until the pilot relieving you can reach the motor controls.

Pilots should carry hankies in a handy place to wipe off goggles.

Riding on the steps, wings, or rail of the machine is prohibited.

In case the engine fails on takeoff, land straight ahead regardless of obstacles.

No machine must taxi faster than a man can walk.

Never run motor so that blast will blow on other machines.

Learn to gauge altitude, especially on landing.

If you see another machine near you, get out of the way.

No two cadets should ever ride together in the same machine.

Do not trust altitude instruments.

Before you begin a landing glide, see that no machines are under you.

Hedge-hopping will not be tolerated.

If flying against the wind and you wish to fly with the wind, don't make a sharp turn near the ground. You may crash.

Motors have been known to stop during a long glide. If pilot wishes to use motor for landing, he should open the throttle.

Don't attempt to force the machine onto the ground with more than flying speed. The result is bounding and ricocheting.

Pilots will not wear spurs while flying.

Do not use aeronautical gasoline in cars or motorcycles.

You must not take off or land closer than fifty feet to the hanger.

Never take a machine into the air until you are familiar with its controls and instruments.

If an emergency occurs while flying, land as soon as possible.

During a reunion of WWI airmen, decorated fighter ace Ole Olsen of Sweden was introduced as a speaker by the MC. During his presentation, Ole was asked by a member of the audience about his most trying moment in battle. "Well," he began, his Nordic accent hanging heavily, "one day, flying over the North Sea, I look behind me, and there's all these Fokkers quickly closing in."

At this point, the obviously distressed MC rushed to the microphone and hastily explained, "Ladies and gentlemen, the Fokker was a warplane used by the German forces."

"Ya," continued Ole, "that's true, but *These* Fokkers were flying Messerschmidts!"

— Ken K

One of my instructors in FE school[93] told me about this.

Apparently the loadmaster[94] (LM) on a USAF C-130[95] was invited to take the engineer's seat for awhile. He started jabbering away, not realizing that he was transmitting on Unicom[96] instead of over the intercom.

LM: "Hey, this is great! I see why you engineers like this seat so much! You can see everything from here! This is just like the starship Enterprise! All ahead, Mr. Sulu, warp factor ten!"

Followed shortly by ATC: "You wanna get back on the intercom, Captain Kirk? You're transmitting on my frequency!"

If you can learn how to fly as a 2nd Lieutenant and not forget how to fly by the time you're a Major, you will have lived a happy life.

Instrument flying is when your mind gets a grip on the fact that there is vision beyond sight.
— U.S. Navy *Approach* magazine circa W.W.II

Without ammunition, the USAF would be just another expensive flying club.

There is no reason to fly through a thunderstorm in peacetime.
— Sign over squadron ops desk at
Davis-Monthan AFB, AZ, 1970

The RF-4E Phantom: living proof that if you put enough engine on something, even a brick can fly.

---

93 Flight Engineer
94 Boss of cargo
95 Large, powerful cargo aircraft
96 Internal communication frequency

This is a rather classic conversation overheard on the radio at an airport just prior to a short landing in a high performance aircraft. The location and the pilot involved shall remain unnamed to protect the guilty!

Tower: "XXXX, cleared to land."

XXXX: "Roger."

Tower: "XXXX, I can't see any landing gear. Is your gear down?"

XXXX: "Say again? I can't hear you because there's some damn horn blaring in my ear!"

Tower: "Your landing gear is *not down*"

XXXX: "Say what??? I can't understand you"

Tower: "*Your landing gear is…. Aw SHIT!*"

If you don't know who the world's greatest fighter pilot is, it ain't you.

There's a story about a C-124[97] and an F-4[98] on intersecting taxiways at Rhein-Main airport (Germany) long ago. The F-4 driver asked Ground what the Globemaster's intentions were.

It's said that the C-124 pilot opened the clamshell doors in the nose and announced, "I'm going to eat you."

— David Fisher, frc@eznet.net

"Back in my early military flying days, I once flew in a two-seat TF-51[99] with a pilot who 'thought' he was pretty hot. He particularly liked to take off, raise a few inches off the runway, pull up the (landing) gear, and hold his altitude while the undercarriage came up.

---

97 Very large cargo aircraft
98 Much smaller multi-purpose combat aircraft
99 Mustang Trainer

Well, on this particular take-off the airplane settled slightly.
It was obvious that the prop tips struck the runway.

I was rattled, but pleased that the airplane was still flying
well enough to climb. But when the pilot contacted departure
control and was obviously continuing on his mission, I was convinced I was with a lunatic.

I asked if he didn't think it would be wise to land and check
the damage and he replied, 'Naw, it's their runway. Let them
worry about it.'"

— Dennis D. Turner, dennis.turner@rmci.net

The job of the Wing Commander is to worry incessantly that
his career depends solely on the abilities of his aviators to fly
their airplanes without mishap and that their only minuscule
contribution to the effort is to bet their lives on it.

It seemed that everybody and his brother arrived back at
Moody AFB[100] at the same time. The frequency was cluttered with
directions to breakout and re-enter, formations breaking up on
the downwind and other challenges to the over-taxed controller.

At the height of the confusion, a T-38 arrived on initial[101].
Aboard was a crew with keen appreciation for the work load
placed on the folks in the tower. Their radio call?

"Moody Tower, Sacker 43 on initial. What are my
intentions?"

Night formation is really an endless series of near misses in
equilibrium with each other.

A military cargo plane flying over a populated area, suddenly loses power and starts to nose down. The pilot tries to

---
100 U.S. Air Force Base
101 First contact

pull up, but with all their cargo, the plane is too heavy. So he yells to the soldiers in back to throw things out to make the plane lighter. They throw out a pistol. "Throw out more!" shouts the pilot. So they throw out a rifle. "More!" he cries again. They heave out a missile, and the pilot regains control. He pulls out of the dive and lands safely at an airport. They get into a jeep and drive off.

Pretty soon they meet a boy on the side of the road who's crying. They ask him why he's crying and he says, "A pistol hit me on the head!"

They drive more and meet another boy who's crying even harder. Again they ask why. The boy says, "A rifle hit me on the head!" They apologize and keep driving.

They meet a boy on the sidewalk who's laughing hysterically. They ask him, "Kid, what's so funny?"

The boy replies, "I farted and a house blew up!"

An Air Force cargo plane was preparing for departure from Thule Air Base in Greenland. They were waiting for the truck to arrive to pump out the aircraft's sewage holding tank.

The aircraft commander was in a hurry, the truck was late in arriving, and the airman performing the job was extremely slow in getting the tank pumped out.

When the commander berated the airman for his slowness and promised punishment, the airman responded, "Sir, I have no stripes, it is twenty below zero, I'm stationed in Greenland, and I'm pumping sewage out of airplanes. Just what are you going to do to punish me?"

According to Reuters, the dazed crew of a Japanese trawler was plucked out of the Sea of Japan clinging to the wreckage of their sunken ship. Their rescue was followed by immediate imprisonment once authorities questioned the sailors on their ship's loss.

To a man, they claimed that a cow, falling out of a clear blue sky, had struck the trawler amidships, shattering its hull and sinking the vessel within minutes. They remained in prison for several weeks until the Russian Air Force reluctantly informed Japanese authorities that the crew of one of its cargo planes had apparently stolen a cow wandering at the edge of a Siberian airfield, forced the cow into the plane's hold, and had hastily taken off for home.

Unprepared for live cargo, the Russian crew was ill-equipped to manage a frightened cow rampaging within the hold.

To save the aircraft and themselves, they shoved the animal out of the cargo hold as they crossed the Sea of Japan at an altitude of 30,000 feet.

When I was working at CFB[102] North Bay, Ontario (home of air defence command and 22nd NORAD[103] Region HQ) I frequently saw pictures of the Bear[104] aircraft that were checking our air defence measures on their way to Cuba from Russia.

Usually the RCAF[105] would scramble two CF-101 Voodoo interceptors to check on the Bear. One would assume the position behind the Bear and the other would fly alongside, taking pictures.

Often, there would be a couple of Russian crewmen in the big round blister near the rear of the aircraft with their cameras taking pictures of our guys taking their pictures.

---

102 Canadian Forces Base
103 North American Aerospace Defense Command
104 Russian bomber
105 Royal Canadian Air Force

One picture that turned out was a Russian airman holding up the centerfold of the current edition of *Playboy*. This one was so current that not even North Bay had their copies yet. The Russian was grinning from ear to ear. Just goes to show you that they had a sense of humor.

Apparently right after a military C-5 Galaxy[106] landed and cleared the active[107], it taxied by a Boeing 757 that was holding short of the runway.

The Galaxy captain, knowing how much larger his aircraft was, keyed the mike and asked the 757 captain, "Hey, little buddy, what's your gross?"

Not to be out-done, the 757 captain keyed his mike and replied, "A little over two hundred thousand dollars a year. How about you?"

Here's another one from the wacky minds of our military controllers at Namao (CFB Edmonton). A bit of background is in order:

Namao is a military field just outside of Edmonton. All aircraft touching down at Namao require a PPR (Prior Permission Request) number, and have to recite it to the controller at first contact. Our flying club is civilian/military, and all our aircraft have permanent PPR's.

One day, we were sitting around listening to the scanner, when a Tomahawk[108] from a local flight school announced inbound for circuits[109]. The controllers asked for the PPR number. The pilot said they didn't know about one. We expected the aircraft to turn

---

106 One of largest aircraft ever made.
107 Active runway
108 Two-seater trainer
109 AKA "touch and goes;" touchdown, then immediately take off without stopping. Practice.

away, but the controller cleared them right-base[110] for 29[111]. We now pick up the audio from this momentous day:

Tomahawk: "F-XAA is final 29, touch and go."

Tower: "XAA is cleared touch and go, 29." (Several more circuits later...)

Tomahawk: "F-XAA is final 29, touch and go."

Tower: "F-XAA is cleared touch and go, 29. How many more circuits were you planning on making?"

Tomahawk: "We thought we'd make one or two more."

Tower: "Roger. I just wondered because we were calculating your landing fees You're up to $13,000 now." (long pause)

Tomahawk: "*That was our last one!*" Another long pause

Tower: "Just kidding. Next time, read your flight supplement."

Air Force Four-Five, it appears your engine has... Oh, disregard.... I see you've already ejected.

"Somebody said that carrier pilots were the best in the world. They must be or there wouldn't be any of them left alive."

— Ernie Pyle

A journalist was doing a report on the reputed sexual prowess of Naval aviators. As part of her investigation she was interviewing an older Captain, supposedly one of the most "active" of all the pilots.

The journalist asked, "When was the last time you had sex?"

"Nineteen fifty-six," the Captain responded after some thought.

---

110 Requires right turn to final approach.
111 Runway number identified by compass direction.

"Excuse me sir, but from what everyone says about your abilities, that sure seems like a long time since you've had sex" the journalist responded.

The Captain shrugged. "Well, it's only twenty thirty-three[112] now," he said, checking his watch.

— Dan Scharf, dscharf@umich.edu

Many years ago when I had the opportunity of taking some cross training with Maritime Command of the RCAF, I chose to fly on an Argus patrol.

An Argus patrol aircraft is a four engine (avgas) prop aircraft derived from the Bristol Brittania. It had the same wings and tail, but the body was a maritime patrol bomber with a large plexiglass nose and radar beneath the nose.

The one trip I remember was off Canada's eastern coast. The exercise was to detect any Russian submarine with the secondary mission of detecting and plotting any Russian spy ship masquerading as a fishing boat. The trip was pretty uneventful for the major part, but we did find a Russian spy ship. There were a lot of Russian fishing vessels, but this boat had so many antennae, you knew it wasn't there for the fishing.

The Navigator suggested I join him in the nose to see first-hand what the crew did to have some fun. The Argus passed over the vessel and proceeded a considerable distance beyond the vessel, made a 180 turn, and descended to about a hundred feet over the water.

The flight engineer had throttled back all the engines, so the props were turning over just enough to keep us airborne. As we were just about to pass over the Russian vessel, just above its antennae, the Nav gave the command to the flight engineer

---

112 8:33 PM by 12 hour clock

for full power. As soon as the power was rammed on, the props gave a huge burst of energy that broke most of the antennae on the ship.

We definitely could see this on our second pass as the seamen were shaking their fists at us while we were laughing. They couldn't put in an official report as they would have to admit just what sort of mission they were on.

Blue water Navy truism: There are more planes in the ocean than submarines in the sky. (From an old carrier sailor)

What's the difference between American pilots and Iraqi pilots?

American pilots break ground and fly into the wind.

"My daddy told a story about my Uncle Bob. Uncle Bob was a pilot in Desert Storm. His plane was hit. He had to bail out over enemy territory. All he had was a small flask of whiskey, a pistol and a survival knife. He drank the whiskey on the way down so it wouldn't break. Then his parachute landed right in the middle of twenty enemy troops.

He shot fifteen until he ran out of bullets, killed four more with the knife 'till the blade broke, then he killed the last Iraqi with his bare hands."

"Good heavens," said the horrified teacher. What kind of moral did your daddy tell you from that horrible story?"

"Stay the hell away from Uncle Bob when he's been drinking!"

A (pre-liberation) Iraqi flying a Mirage F1 came upon a US EF-111A Raven at low level and pursued it.

As a bit of background for this; the Mirage is a reasonably decent aircraft at low level, but the EF-111A is something else. It's an unarmed electronic warfare version of the F-111 Aardvark. It has terrain following radar, which enables it to fly at Mach[113] 1 or more, two hundred feet above the ground (that's about 0.4 seconds from it), while the pilot watches the view. It's one of the fastest aircraft in the world at low level.

Maybe this Iraqi didn't know anything about the F-111, but he decided that it looked like an easy target and pursued it at very low level.

The EF-111 crew was credited with a kill when the Iraqi (not surprisingly) slammed into the ground.

There can't be too many occasions when an unarmed aircraft scores a kill.

When Hillary Clinton visited Iraq, the Army Blackhawk helicopter used to transport the Senator was given the call sign "Broomstick One."

And they say the Army has no sense of humor!

A military aircraft had gear problems on landing. As the plane was skidding down the tarmac, the tower controller asked if they needed assistance. From the plane came a laconic Southern drawl: "Dunno, we ain't done crashin' yet."

SR-71 BLACKBIRD[114]

In his book, *Sled Driver*, SR-71 Blackbird pilot Brian Shul writes:

I'll always remember a certain radio exchange that occurred one day as Walt (my back-seater) and I were screaming across Southern California thirteen miles high. We were monitoring

---

113 Speed of sound
114 Very high speed, very high altitude aircraft

various radio transmissions from other aircraft as we entered Los Angeles airspace. Although they didn't really control us, they did monitor our movement across their scope.

I heard a Cessna ask for a readout of its ground speed. "Ninety knots," Center replied. Moments later, a Twin Beech requested the same. "120 knots," Center answered.

We weren't the only ones proud of our ground speed that day as almost instantly an F-18 smugly transmitted, "Ah, Center, Dusty 52 requests ground speed readout." There was a slight pause, then the response, "525 knots on the ground, Dusty."

Another pause.

As I was thinking how ripe a situation this was, I heard a familiar click of a radio transmission coming from my back-seater. It was at that precise moment I realized Walt and I had become a real crew, for we were both thinking in unison.

"Center, Aspen 20, you got a ground speed readout for us?" There was a longer than normal pause.

"Aspen, I show 1,742 knots." (That's about 2005 mph)

No further inquiries were heard on that frequency.

Several years ago I heard a pilot check in with a southern Approach Control. He said with an exaggerated Southern drawl:

"Birdseed Approach, Barnburner 123 with you at seven thousand, with Information, excuse the expression, Yankee."

In another famous SR-71 story, Los Angeles Center reported receiving a request for clearance to FL 600 (60,000 ft).

The incredulous controller, with some disdain in his voice, asked, "How do you plan to get up to 60,000 feet?

The pilot (obviously a sled driver), responded, "We don't plan to go up to it. We plan to come down to it."

He was cleared.

"You know the part in *High Flight* where it talks about putting out your hand to touch the face of God? Well, when we're at speed and altitude in the SR, we have to slow down and descend to do that."

> — USAF Lt. Col. Gil Bertelson, SR-71 pilot, in *SR-71 Blackbird: Stories, Tales and Legends*, 2002

Though I Fly Through the Valley of Death, I Shall Fear No Evil For I am at 80,000 Feet and Climbing! (Sign over the entrance to the old SR-71 operating base at Kadena, Japan)

"The cockpit was my office. It was a place where I experienced many emotions and learned many lessons. It was a place of work, but also a keeper of dreams. It was a place of deadly serious encounters, yet there I discovered much about life.

"I learned about joy and sorrow, pride and humility, fear and overcoming fear. I saw much from that office that most people would never see. At times it terrified me, yet I could always feel at home there. It was my place, at that time in space, and the jet was mine for those moments.

Though it was a place where I could quickly die, the cockpit was a place where I truly lived."

> — Brian Shul, *Sled Driver: Flying The World's Fastest Jet*

"You've never been lost until you've been lost at Mach 3."

> — Paul F. Crickmore, SR-71 test pilot

SEVENTEEN

Control Tower

In a holding pattern behind several aircraft.

Pilot: "Request an estimate for our clearance for the approach."

Controller: "Bonanza 1234, is there a problem?"

Pilot: "Do the words, 'Daddy, I gotta go potty!' mean anything to you?"

Controller: "Bonanza 1234, cleared for approach."

Airline 123: "Airline 123, request a 360[115] to parking."

Ground: "360 approved, 180 recommended."

[pause]

Airline 123: "You've been saving that one for while, haven't you?"

A pilot on final approach is having difficulty. The controller rolls out the equipment (emergency) and radios the pilot to ask if there's anything else they can do for him.

The plaintive reply, "Call my insurance agent."

---

115 Degrees of turn.

Many commercial aircraft are stacked up waiting for approach to O'Hare International. ATC has inflicted numer

ous delays. Some planes are already one to two hours late. The weather is good. It's just that there's a traffic volume bottleneck. Pilots, passengers, crews are all getting quite frustrated and angry.

ATC: "All aircraft holding, expect twenty minutes additional delay."

Unknown A/C: "Ahhh…, bullshit!"

ATC: "Aircraft making last transmission, identify yourself."

(silence)

ATC: "Aircraft making last transmission, identify yourself immediately!"

(silence)

ATC: "Aircraft using 'bullshit' in last transmission, identify yourself. American 411, was that you?"

American 411: "Approach, American 411. Negative on the 'bullshit,' sir."

Northwest 202: "Approach, Northwest 202. Negative on the 'bullshit."

Delta 55: "Approach, Delta 55. Negative on the 'bullshit."

Northwest 33: "Approach, Northwest 33. We have a negative on that 'bullshit." And so on, right through the entire pattern[116].

The controller, who was working a busy pattern, told the 727 on downwind to make a three-sixty (do a complete circle, usually to provide spacing between aircraft).

---

116 Lots of traffic

The pilot of the 727 complained, "Do you know it costs us five hundred dollars to make a three-sixty in this airplane?

Without missing a beat the controller replied, "Roger. Give me a thousand dollars worth, NOW!"

This happened at the Boston ARTCC[117] where I work. The controller noticed that a jet wasn't going to make the 11,000-foot crossing restriction required by Providence Approach. As the controller was issuing the "expedite" clearance to get him down, he noticed the jet also had head-on traffic at 15,000. His clearance went like this:

"Flight XXX, expedite your descent to 11,000, but *really* expedite through 14,000."

A DC-10 had an exceedingly long roll out after landing because both his approach and landing speeds were a little hot.

San Jose Tower: "American 751 heavy, turn right at the end, if able. If unable, take the Guadeloupe exit off of Highway 101 and make a right at the light to return to the airport."

I have a Helio Courier which is a STOL[118] airplane that can fly at very low airspeeds. On approach to my home airport, I was flying slowly down the 5,000-foot runway to the end where my hangar is. With a stiff headwind, I probably had a ground speed below fifteen knots.

Finally, an exasperated tower controller said, "Helio Courier on 24 Left, could you please just land and taxi to your hangar? It'd be quicker."

---

117 Air Route Traffic Control Center
118 Short Take-Off and Landing

DCA[119] clearance delivery responded to a request for an IFR clearance with a rapid-fire clearance that went on and on, with various VOR[120]s, fixes, altitudes, etc.

After a pause, a voice came back, in a slow Texas drawl, "Okay. Now why don't you 'all say that again, real slow, as if it mattered."

— Vincent Norris

"Cessna One Alpha Bravo, you've unidentified traffic at two o'clock, three miles, altitude unknown, over the railroad tracks. Very slow moving primary target. Might be a helicopter."

(Long pause)

"Might be a train."

ATC to Flight 123: "Slow to 300 knots, please." After several moments, it was apparent the crew hadn't complied with the first speed reduction and was overtaking the inbound plane ahead of them.

ATC to Flight 123: "Slow to 280 knots." This was soon followed by a request for 250 knots from ATC when the crew still hadn't slowed the airplane.

Finally, the now-frustrated controller ordered, "Gentlemen, the number is 250. Either slow to it or turn to it!"

— www.aviation-humor.com

It was a really nice day, right about dusk. A Piper Malibu was being vectored into a long line of airliners to land at Kansas City.

---

119 Reagan National
120 Navigation Aid

KC Approach: "Malibu three-two-Charlie, you're following a 727, one o'clock and three miles."

Three-two-Charlie: "We've got him. We'll follow him."

KC Approach: "Delta 105 (the 727); your traffic to follow is a Malibu, eleven o'clock and three miles. Do you have that traffic?"

Delta 105 (long pause, then in a thick Southern drawl): "Well.... I've got something down there. Can't quite tell if it's a Malibu or a Chevelle, though."

On my first solo cross-country, I was flying north through the San Fernando Valley, trying to keep track of traffic callouts. Apparently there was a controller with a similar problem.

He had managed to confuse a commercial jet on approach to Burbank with a private plane transitioning south across the valley. For a period of about ninety seconds, he was calling out instructions to them, but wasn't quite sure what he wanted.

Finally the commercial jet pilot inquired as to where he was being sent.

There was a brief exchange about intentions, followed by an "Oops" and thirty seconds of silence.

The next voice I heard on that frequency said, "Attention, all aircraft. Previous controller no longer a factor[121]."

I overheard this while on ground control in MIA[122].

Virgin Flight: "Every time we come to MIA, you women controllers give us a hard time."

ATC: "For the nine years I've been a controller, I've never had a problem handling a Virgin."

— DoogieATP@aol.com

---

121 A "factor" is something that may negatively affect operations.
122 Miami Airport

Unknown Aircraft: "I'm f**king bored!"

Air Traffic Control: "Last aircraft transmitting, identify yourself *immediately!*"

Unknown Aircraft: "I said I was f**king bored, not f**king stupid!"

As a young co-pilot, I used to enjoy getting traffic advisories by center that involved Fokker Jets. I just got a kick out of saying, "I've got that Fokker visual" or "BUFF-21 has the Fokker in sight" because it sounded similar to another word I tend to use too often.

On one sortie, after I made my "Fokker visual" call, my captain flipped out, believing I had said the profanity and not "Fokker." In his anger he pressed *down* on the interphone/radio switch and broadcast on the UHF radio instead of *up* for the interphone and said, "You didn't just say f**ker on the radio did you?"

Before I could respond Ft. Worth center came back with a, "No, but you just did."

I was in tears.

"If God had intended man to fly, He would not have invented Spanish Air Traffic Control."

— Lister, in the BBC TV series, *Red Dwarf*

I was a Pan Am 727 Flight Engineer waiting for start clearance in Munich, Germany. I was listening to the radio since I was the junior crew member. This was the conversation I overheard:

Lufthansa: (In German) "Ground, what is our start clearance time?"

Ground: (In English) "If you want an answer, you must speak English."

Lufthansa: (In English) "I am a German, flying a German airplane, in Germany. Why must I speak English?"

Before Ground could answer, someone with a beautiful English accent said: "Because you lost the bloody war!"

A colleague of mine was dealing with a particularly difficult private pilot. The pilot had been having a hard time following instructions. I could tell he was nervous and flustered. While flying on a northwesterly heading of 310, the controller told him to turn right to heading 360.

The pilot asked, "Are you sure you want me to turn *right* to heading three-six-zero?"

The controller didn't miss a beat and replied, "Well, sir, I assumed you were facing forward in the cockpit."

— Gary Ryle, Orlando International Airport

True conversation heard at Hannover Airport.

The young woman in the Tower has recently finished her training and is still not completely at ease. BA[123] 123 is at holding position for runway 09R. Another aircraft is doing approach procedures for a landing on the same runway. Tower wishes to expedite take-off for BA 123:

Tower: "BA 123, are you ready for a quickie?"

BA 123: "Lady, I'm always ready for a quickie, but first I have to fly this plane to Helsinki!"

A pilot planning a VFR flight was getting a weather briefing from AFSS[124]. When told of a line of thunderstorms approaching the departure airport the pilot asked, "Well, if I'm IFR, will the thunderstorms still be there?"

---

123 British Air
124 Flight Service Station: automated

The weather in Oregon has been seasonal; rain for days and snow starting yesterday. Freezing down to 2000 feet. I'm based at the Illinois Valley Airport (3S4), Cave Junction, OR, surrounded by the beautiful Siskiyou Mountains.

I've been waiting to ferry a PA-32 to Southern California. Yesterday morning I called Flight Service and asked for an outlook briefing to get over the Siskiyous southbound. The FSS[125] Specialist asked, "And what month are you planning to depart?"

Overheard recently on the ground control frequency at Midway Airport (MDW) in Chicago:

Vanguard 123: "Midway Ground, Vanguard 123 request push back from Gate 6."

MDW Ground: "Vanguard 123, push back approved. Point your nose toward the city."

Vanguard 123: "Vanguard 123, Wilco."

Then, a couple of minutes later:

MDW Ground: "Vanguard 123, just which city did you think I was talking about?"

Tampa Approach: "CAP Flight 567, you have traffic at your six o'clock position, one mile, same altitude."

CAP Flight 567: "Roger, Tampa, we don't have rear-view mirrors installed, so please keep us informed."

Apparently the controllers were getting annoyed with the Air Canada pilots who regularly flew into Winnipeg. It would seem that the source of the irritation was the tone of voice that these guys were using. They would come on the frequency with the deepest voices you could imagine, saying things like, "This is Air Canada 345 heavy with Whiskey for Runway 18."

---

125 Flight Service Station: manned

One of the controllers finally had had enough of this sort of affectation and decided to get even. One day he went out and bought a bunch of helium filled balloons.

Sure enough, the first Air Canada flight to arrive in the airspace checked in with the big deep pilot voice. The controller took a huge honk of the helium and cleared the flight to land in a voice akin to Donald Duck wearing very tight shorts!

No one was sure how the pilots reacted, but it gave the controllers one heck of a high!

ACA1147: "Moncton, Air Canada 1147, can you get the winds from 167 above us?"

CZQM: "As soon as I get a chance, I will."

(some time passes with continuous radio chatter)

ACA1147: "Moncton, 1147, what are his winds up there?"

CZQM: "Standby for that, please."

(more radio chatter)

ACA1147: "Moncton, can you ask company 167 for his winds?"

CZQM: "Okay, 1147 and 167, I have a little too much to do for that sort of thing right now. I'll leave it up to you guys to go over to the company frequency and pass winds."

Pilot: "Tower, Cessna 1234, what's the wind doing?"

Tower: "Blowing." (Laughter in background)

Overheard after a Lear's very steep climb out of Teterboro:

Controller: "Lear 1234, after retrieving your passengers from the tail section, contact departure."

Conducting fuel-consumption tests on a new twin-engine plane, we were en route from Pennsylvania to Florida. Just north of Richmond, VA, I called the air-traffic controller to make a position report on our plane, whose designation was 5000Y. The controller, in a Southern drawl, replied, "Oh, no, not again!"

I was puzzled by the response until I realized what I had said, "We are 5000 Yankee, 25 miles north of Richmond."

— Joe Diblin

Cessna 1234: "Fifteen miles from VORTAC[126]. Request a VOR, Runway 14 approach, circle to land, full stop."

Approach: "Cessna 1234, say your indicated airspeed."

Cessna 1234: "Our ground speed is 59 knots. Is that going to be a problem?"

Approach: "No problem. We're open 24 hours."

Tower: "Have you got enough fuel or not?"
Pilot: "Yes."
Tower: "Yes, what?"
Pilot: "Yes, *SIR.*"

A conversation involving a motor-glider being flown to a local airport for some repair work on a noisy muffler:
Control tower: "You're unreadable, say again."
Glider: "I've turned off the engine. Is that better?"
Control Tower: silence

A pilot overheard this exchange between another pilot and a female controller at Miami Center:

---

126 Navigational Aid

Cessna 1234: "Miami Center, this is Cessna 1234. Are you having radio problems? We're hearing intermittent static on your frequency."

Miami Center: "Yeah, my husband says he gets intermittent static from me, too."

A 727 was on a scheduled service run into Orlando descending below 15,000 feet.

During one three-minute span, the aircraft received five "vector for traffic"[127] calls from Approach Control. Upon receiving the sixth, the Captain asked, "Are we the only ones up here with ailerons[128] today?"

Cessna 123: "Tower, I have a load of Young Eagles on board. Do you have any idea how long I should keep them up here?"

Tower: "Cessna 123, Ahhh, until the second one throws up. That should just about do it."

N124: "Youngstown Approach, Cessna 124. Request two practice ILS approaches, followed by a VOR to hold, a VOR approach, two NDB[129] approaches, and an ASR[130] approach."

Approach: "Cessna 124 squawk[131] 4753, and would you like fries with that, sir?"

Overheard on Ft. Smith, AR, Approach frequency:

Cherokee 1234: "Cherokee 1234 requesting direct Paris."

Razorback Approach: "Cherokee 1234. Is that Paris, AR, or Paris, TX? It's kinda important."

---

127 Change flight path to avoid other aircraft.
128 Control surfaces at trailing edge of wings.
129 Non-directional Beacon
130 Airport Surveillance Radar
131 Identification Friend or Foe (IFF) setting

München[132] II Tower: "LH[133] 8610 cleared for take-off."

Pilot (LH 8610): "But we've not even landed."

Tower: "Who's that standing at 26 South?"

Pilot (LH 8801): "LH 8801."

Tower: "Okay, then *you're* cleared for take-off."

When President Bush was in residence at his ranch in Crawford, TX, the prohibited area around it expanded. Pilots were instructed by NOTAM[134] to contact nearby Waco approach control for assistance in avoiding the airspace.

While flying in the area, a pilot monitoring frequency overheard the following from the very busy Waco controller:

"Cessna 1234, don't be alarmed by the two F-16s circling a couple of thousand feet overhead, but *DO NOT* climb until advised."

A light twin had just landed on Runway 29. Missing the last turnoff onto Taxiway Delta[135], the pilot started to turn left onto Golf when the controller spoke up:

Tower: "N1234, that taxiway is approved for single-engine use only."

N1234: "That's okay. I'll just shut down one engine."

PIA[136]: "TWA 686, how's the ride?"

TWA 686: "It's rougher than burlap underwear up here."

PIA, after a short pause to catch a breath: "Would you classify that as light, moderate, or severe chafing?"

---

132 Munich, Germany

133 Lufthanza abbreviation

134 Notice to Airmen - special conditions

135 Taxiways are identified with phonetic name, runways by compass heading.

136 Peoria, IL

Salt Lake Center, (ZSL) was trying to raise Delta Airlines Flight 444:

(numerous times): "Delta 444, Salt Lake Center."

Finally, Delta 444 answered: "Salt Lake, Delta 444. Sorry about that. We were in the back watching the movie."

Unknown: "What's playing?"

Delta 444: "Lost in space."

The local weather was 1,700 feet broken-to-overcast with eight miles visibility underneath, an improvement from the 800 overcast that had prevailed most of the morning. As I motored along above the clouds, I heard the following:

"Approach, this is Cessna 456. We need some help getting down."

Approach: "Can you fly IFR?"

Cessna 456: "Nope."

Approach: "Are you VFR right now?"

Cessna 456: "Nope."

(Protracted silence)

Approach: "Can you hold a heading and altitude?"

Cessna 456: "No problemo."

Approach: "Stay on your current heading and altitude until you reach VFR conditions."

Cessna 456: "Roger."

Approach: "When you get to VFR, let's talk."

Cessna 456: "About what?"

Approach: "I'm sure we can think of something."

One night while climbing out on a single-engine IFR flight:

N6851R: "Denver, Centurion 6851 Romeo, checking in out of twelve (thousand) for FL180[137]."

---

137 Flight Level 18,000 feet

Center: "51 Romeo, radar contact fifty miles east of the Denver VOR". (pause)

N6851R: "Uh, Denver, 51 Romeo. Sir, I show us fifty miles *west* of Denver VOR."

Center: "51 Romeo, Correction. Make that 24,950 miles east of the Denver VOR."

Center: "Delta 999, say your speed for in-trail spacing."

Delta 999: "Center, oh, we're really hauling ass."

Center: "I don't care what kind of cargo you're carrying. I just want to know how fast you're going."

Heard on the frequency while going into Newark, NJ (EWR) a while back:

Heavy jet: "Left to 120, and if it helps, we've got the field."

NY TRACON[138]: "Roger. Let me know when you get the twelve guys ahead of you in sight."

While recently flying from FLL[139] to JFK, an airline captain was given holding instructions due to congestion. After holding for quite some time, the captain finished an exchange with a controller with an attempt to clarify his situation:

Captain: "Copy. Could we get an EFC [expect further clearance], please?"

ATC: "Indefinite."

Captain: "I don't think I have the fuel for that."

Late one dark and cloudy night, I was flying northward across central California. As Bakersfield Approach handed me

---

138 Terminal Radar Approach Control
139 Ft. Lauderdale, FL

over to LA Center the controller said, "You're about to leave my airspace and the known world."

Tower: "Airline XXX, it looks like one of your baggage doors is open."

Captain (after quickly scanning the FE[140] panel): "Ah, thanks Tower, but you must be looking at our APU[141] door."

Tower: "Okay, Airline XXX, cleared for takeoff."

Captain: "Cleared for takeoff, Airline XXX."

Tower, during the takeoff roll: "Airline XXX, Ahh... It appears that your APU is leaking luggage."

Cessna G684: "Request taxi clearance to Kelowna."

Ground: "Cessna G684, we'd prefer if you flew there."

Cessna G684: "Then we request taxi clearance to the active."

One C-172 couldn't seem to do anything right. Finally the exasperated controller shook his finger at the Cessna and hollered, "Don't make me come up there."

Veep Al Gore's delayed departure from ALB[142] on a Friday night snarled air traffic in the northeast. After yet another revised EFC, ATC queried one hardy soul on his status:

ALB Approach: "Commuter 5678, can you hold out for another half hour or so?"

Commuter 5678: "Yes, sir, fuel is not a problem. But I should advise you that about half my passengers have now turned Republican."

---

140 Flight Engineering Panel
141 Auxiliary Power Unit
142 Albany, NY

Cessna: "Van Nuys Ground, Cessna 2467 Sierra. How do you read[143]?"

Ground: "On about a twelfth-grade level." (followed by laughter in the background)

Cessna 152 pilot with obvious French accent: "Center, I'd like a vector back home."

Unidentified commuter pilot: "Heading 090, 2000 miles."

Overworked air traffic controller responding to the disoriented student pilot of a single-engine Cessna who's calling him on 121.5 MHz (emergency frequency) on a busy Saturday afternoon: "Lost aircraft, say position."

Another controller, working departure radar one night, issued a warning to a Braniff Boeing 720 that had just taken off.

"Traffic twelve o'clock, three miles, several targets, possibly a flight of ducks."

The pilot responded by asking, "Do those ducks paint (appear on the radarscope) better if they're banded?"

To which the controller responded, "No, but it'd sure help if they had a transponder." The Braniff pilot then quipped, "Well, they squawk[144], don't they?"

— Bill Owen (retired), Portland International Airport

A female controller was training on local when an inbound pilot asked her to "kill the rabbit." Noticing her confusion, the instructor explained that she should turn off the white

---

143 Quality of reception
144 Transmit IFF code

approach lights that flash in sequence, much like a hare scampering down the runway.

Later in her training, the controller was working local again and decided to try to impress her peers. Confidently keying the mike, she asked another inbound pilot, "Would you like me to choke the chicken?"

The pilot, no doubt in hysterics, was unable to reply.

— Mark Nighswonger, Springfield, IL Tower

Several of us "old hands" were sitting in the tower on a relatively slow afternoon with a trainee working ground control. Out on the ramp, an old Convair 440 turboprop[145] began running up its engines for a maintenance check. Suddenly, the trainee jumped up and excitedly pointed to the clouds of blue smoke mushrooming from the No. 1 engine.

We looked over, chuckling, and explained to our charge that all Convairs and other old radial engine planes emit smoke when they start up or the engine floods.

We just about had the newbie calmed down and back in his seat when, of course, the Convair pilot hollered on the radio that he was on fire!

Thankfully, the fire trucks were close.

— Don Tedrow, Austin, TX Tower

Holding for New York

After a passenger suffered a medical emergency, the pilot asked ATC for clearance to land at the nearest available airport. A few moments later, he advised that the passenger had died and asked to proceed to the flight's original destination of La Guardia. The controller advised there was a hold for LGA.

---

145 Gas turbine drives propeller

Fifteen minutes passed while several other aircraft checked in on that frequency, several of which also began holding for LGA. After twenty minutes, the first pilot asked how much longer they'd be holding, adding that "some of the passengers are getting nervous about the dead body on board."

Whereupon another pilot radioed, "How long have you been holding?"

— Scott Straub, Washington Center

The pilot of a small freight/mail plane was getting a little complacent in his phraseology, probably because of the rather dull routine of his late-night run. Every weekday at 0215 he would stop at a small airport and check in with, "Good morning, Jones field, guess who?"

The lone controller was bored, too, but insisted on proper terminology. He would lecture the pilot on proper radio technique every morning. The lectures fell on deaf ears. The pilot continued his daily, "guess who?"

That is, until the morning that again the radio crackled, "Jones Field, guess who?"

The controller, well prepared, turned off all the lights on the airport and responded, "Jones Field, guess *where!*" establishing proper communications from then on.

Tower: "12345, are you a Cessna?"
12345: "No. I'm a male Hispanic."

ATC: "N123YZ, say altitude."
N123YZ: "*Altitude!*"
ATC: "N123YZ, say airspeed."
N123YZ: "*Airspeed!*"
ATC: "N123YZ, say cancel IFR."
N123YZ: "Eight thousand feet, one hundred fifty knots indicated!"

Extracted from the UK CAA GASIL (general aviation safety info leaflet) Dec 1991:

Lady Radar Controller: "Can I turn you on at seven miles?"

Airline Captain: "Madam, you can try."

Pilot: "Golf Juliet Whiskey, request instructions for take-off."

Person unknown: "Open the throttle smoothly, check temperatures and pressures rising, keep the aircraft straight using…"

Pilot: "Tower, please call me a fuel truck."

Tower: "Roger. You're a fuel truck."

And one from Daytona, Florida:

"Tower, this is N123ER, how do you read?"

"Usually at night, in bed, with my light on."

And from Sydney, Australia:

"Hold your push back Qantas. You've got a Virgin with a tight slot behind you."

An air-traffic controller at a small private airport was working on a wintry day when the temperature was -30°, the wind-chill factor was -55°, and it was blowing snow.

The pilot of a small plane called for landing instructions. His aircraft number was unfamiliar, so, not knowing his destination at the airport, the controller asked, "Where would you like to park, sir?"

His warm Southern drawl came through the frigid air loud and clear, "Miami!"

Its night over Las Vegas, information Hotel is current, but Mooney 33W is unfamiliar and talking to Approach Control.

Approach: "33 Whiskey, confirm you have Hotel."

33W: "Uhhhmm, We're flying into McCarren International. Uhhhmm, but we don't have a room yet."

Approach control was laughing too hard to respond. The next several calls went like this:

Approach: "United 5, descend to FL220."

United 5: "United 5 down to FL220. We don't have a hotel room either."

"If you hear me, traffic no longer a factor."

"You're gonna have to key the mike. I can't see when you nod your head."

"Put your compass on 'E' (East) and get out of my airspace!"

"Caution, wake turbulence. You're following a heavy; twelve o'clock, three... No, let's make it five miles."

"Climb like you're life depends on it, 'cause it does."

"If you want more room, Captain, push your seat back."

"Air Force One, I told you to expedite."

"Listen up, gentlemen, or something's gonna happen that none of us wants to see. Besides that, you're pissing me off!"

"The traffic at nine o'clock's gonna do a little Linda Ronstadt on you."

"Linda Ronstadt? What's that?"

"Well, sir, they're gonna 'Blue Bayou.'"

"Approach, X Air 525. What's this aircraft doing at my altitude?"

"X Air 525, what makes you think it's *your* altitude, Captain?"

"How far behind traffic are we?"

"Three miles."

"That doesn't look like three miles to us!"

"You're a mile and a half from him. He's a mile and a half from you. That's three miles."

"Approach, how far from the airport are we in minutes?"

"X Air 923, the faster you go, the quicker you'll get here."

"Midwest Express 726, sorry about that. Center thought you were a Midway arrival. Just sit back, relax, and pass out some more cookies.[146] We'll get you to Milwaukee."

"Approach, what's our sequence?"

"Aircraft calling for the sequence. I missed your call sign, but if I find out what it is, you're last."

"Approach, XYZ Air 436, you want us to turn right to 090?"

"No, I want your brother to turn. Just do it and don't argue."

During November of 1996, Mythical Air added jet bridges to its G concourse. The long bridges were carried into the airport by cranes (which have no radios), leading to this strange transmission:

"X Air 123, give way[147] to the jet bridge. We're not talking to him."

---

146 Midwest bakes cookies on board.
147 Usually means hold for another aircraft moving across your path.

Pilot: "Radar, this is Cessna 4675."

Radar: "Cessna 4675, go ahead."

Pilot: "Radar, I don't seem to be making much progress here. How's my ground speed?"

Radar: "Well, all depends. If you're a hang glider[148], you're doing very well."

Pilot: "Outer marker, inbound."

Tower: "Roger, cleared to land; winds 270 at 21, gusting 29, heavy rain, severe turbulence below 300, RVR[149] 2,000 feet."

Pilot: "Roger. Cleared to land; and oh, let us know if it gets any worse."

Tower: "*Worse?*"

We once had a pilot call in and say "Help, I'm hopelessly lost over Gravette, AR."

We all looked at each other, and after a chuckle, the controller for that area asked the pilot: "If you're hopelessly lost, how do you know you're over Gravette, AR?"

The pilot said, "Because I'm circling the water tank. It says Gravette, AR!" (The town was too small to be on his sectionals)[150].

A pilot called in and said he was unsure of his position, but he had a town in sight. Since he wasn't on radar, the controller told him to descend and look for the town's water tower, see what it says on the side, then climb back up, and tell him.

---

148 Kite-like contraption under which someone hangs after jumping from a height.
149 Runway Visual Range
150 Maps for small and medium aircraft flying VFR.

Sure enough, in about three minutes the pilot called back and said, "Approach, I found the water tower." The controller, looking rather pleased, asked, "And what did it say on the side?"

The pilot replied, "It said Seniors, 1978." Truly happened.

An old-timer is working USA 553 westbound and is about to turn him over to Cleveland.

Controller: "USA 353. Contact Cleveland Center 135.6."

Controller: "USA 353. Contact Cleveland Center 135.6!"

Controller: "USA 353. You're just like my wife. You never listen!"

Pilot: "Center, this is USA 553. Maybe if you called her by the right name, you'd get a better response!"

Tower: "Delta Oscar Mike, squawk 0476."

Pilot: "Say again."

Tower: "Squawk 0476."

Pilot: "Four, zero…?"

Tower: "Do you need an easier one?"

Tower: "Mission triple-three, do you have problems?"

Pilot: "I think I've lost my compass."

Tower: "Judging the way you're flying, you lost the whole instrument panel."

The controller couldn't get the B737 to reduce speed. After three tries using perfect phraseology, the controller finally decides to try something else.

"Airliner 737, are you checked out in a 747?"

"Uh, no. Why?"

"Well, if you don't slow down, you'll be in the cockpit of the one in front of you!"

— Andrew Epstein, AndrewEpstein@
mindspring.com

An American pilot flying a Gulfie 11 was approaching Dublin Airport, Ireland, obviously for the first time. He contacted Dublin Centre to inquire about visibility at the airport. The controller confirmed that the visibility was fine.

Some five minutes later, the Gulfie pilot called again and asked for confirmation that the visibility at Dublin was good. The controller reassured him that Dublin was clear, with no fog.

A third request from the American seeking an update on the visibility at Dublin and the presence of any fog was met by an initial stony silence, followed by, "November blank blank blank. Dublin Airport never gets foggy. *Unless It's Badly Provoked!*"

— Liam Byrne, lpbyrne@indigo.ie

This is not a joke. I heard this on Feb. 14th, 1997, when I was flying from LEE (Leesburg, FL) to TIX (Titusville, FL) in a C172, aircraft number N5456D:

ATC: "Piper N4444D, traffic at your two o'clock, 500 feet below you."

Piper N4444D: "Well, we see a light coming toward us."

ATC: "Look again. There's probably a plane behind that light."

— Karl Heinz Schmid

It was the time in the Soviet Union that communism and central control were natural aspects of everyday life. One day, there was a Tupolev 154 on short final to Oslo Airport. There's a large field close to the runway. The tower controller alerted the pilots:

"Check the farmers on the right side of the runway."

"They're all working," the Soviet pilot responded with a clear Russian accent.

— Tore Kielland, kiellan@telepost.no

At London Gatwick, an Air France A320 is making an auto-approach. At 200 feet, the computer decided to make a go-around with no reason and no command from the crew. Here's what we heard on the Tower freq:

Air France: "London from Air France 1234, it's going around!"

London Twr: "Air France 1234, report intentions."

Air France: "Well... to go with it, sir!"

It was a quiet morning in the control tower at the airport where I was working. I was in the tower. My friend was on ground control. One of the small commuters had just landed. As they taxied to the ramp, the female pilot hit the wrong button and her "Thank you for flying with XYZ Airlines" message went out on the ground control frequency instead of the intercom.

My friend heard this, made an assumption, then made the following broadcast on his frequency, "Attention, all airlines. Someone has a flight attendant talking on the radio."

One of the first space shuttle flights. The Shuttle Columbia above Spain:

Columbia: "Saragosso Tower, this is Columbia. How do you read me?"

Saragosso Tower: "Read you five by five[151]. What's your call sign?"

---

151 Means transmission is full strength, very clear.

Columbia: "Columbia."

Saragosso Tower: "What's your altitude?"

Columbia: "One zero, zero, zero, zero, zero, zero, zero."

The University of North Dakota trains pilots for Air China. Most coming from China speak no English and have had little experience with technology.

I was waiting for departure on the runway at Grand Forks with a UND/Air China training aircraft in front of me.

The tower called the aircraft and asked if it had current information Whiskey.

After a long pose, a Chinese voice replied, "No, no alcohol on board."

— Steveair@aol.com

Overheard during a high volume period at Cleveland:

Tower: "Citation Zero Golf Charlie, cross Five Right, hold short Five Left."

Citation: "Cross Five Left, hold short Five Right."

Tower: "Ya got it backwards."

Citation: "Dyslexia is hard to correct."

Tower: "Yeah, five out of two pilots have it."

— *Real Humor,* by Don Auble, Cleveland, OH (IFR, July 2000)

This Japanese airlines plane is approaching Honolulu International when the tower gives the pilot a clearance he's not familiar with. So he says, "ATC, could you please walk me through that clearance? It's been a while since I was here last."

ATC: "Oh, yeah. When were you here last?"

Pilot: "December 7, 1941."

Tower: "Delta Mike Zulu. After landing, cleared to taxi Alpha seven, Alpha five, Whiskey two, Delta one, and Oscar two."

Pilot: "Where the hell's that? We're not that familiar with this airport."

Tower: "Don't worry. I'm new here, too."

A/C: "Hey, that altimeter setting we got put us fifteen feet underground!"

Tower: "Well, up periscope and taxi to the ramp!"

Controller to transitioning aircraft: "Do you have Miami's altimeter?"

Student pilot (after long pause): "No, sir. This one belongs to the flight school where I rented the plane."

I was taxiing out to the active in a C172. I had just dialed up tower and checked the approach, which was clear. The weather was 15+[152] visibility and no ceiling. I was just about to call tower for clearance when I heard this:

ABC: "London tower, this is Alpha Bravo Charlie on short final to 33."

Tower: "Alpha Bravo Charlie, negative visual contact. Pull up, go around."

I took a good hard look for the aircraft and saw nothing, so I called Tower and got cleared to go. I heard two more renditions of the "On short final" and "Pull up, go around" act.

On the fourth try the pilot got a bit frustrated about the wave off. It went like this:

Tower: "Negative visual contact. Pull up and go around."

ABC: "Well, look out your window. I'm bloody right in front of you!"

---

152 Fifteen miles visibility sometimes called Severe Clear.

The Tower came back cool and collected. "Alpha Bravo Charlie, look down into the centre of the runway. Do you see a big white radar dome?"

ABC: "Err…, negative radar dome."

Tower: "That's because you're not over London. You're over Waterloo-Wellington fifty miles northeast of my position. Waterloo-Wellington's tower frequency is 125.00. I think they'd like to talk to you."

DFW[153] Tower: "Lonestar 189, clear to land 18 Right, wind calm."

Lonestar: "Roger, cleared to land 18 Right."

Lonestar: "Tower, we hit something."

DFW Tower: "*You did what?*"

Lonestar: "We hit a small animal or something on the runway. You know, some sort of road kill or something."

DFW Tower: "UPS 31 Heavy, be advised company that just landed ahead of you on Runway 18 Right reports hitting some sort of road kill."

UPS 31: "That's all right. We'll flatten it out a little bit for ya!"

A friend of mine works for Mesaba Air and relates a radio call he heard at MSP[154]. A female Northwest Airlines cockpit crew member had called several times for push-back clearance.

After receiving the okay, she called back and canceled. Her last request went something like this:

NW123: "Ground control, NW123 ready for push back, again."

---

153 Dallas/Ft. Worth
154 Minneapolis, St. Paul

Ground Control: "Are you sure?"

NW123: "Well, I'm a female and can change my mind at any moment."

Ground Control (laughing): "Cleared to push back."

While flying through Pennsylvania one day under Severe Clear conditions, I overheard this on the radio:

Flight Check 1234: "Harrisburg Approach, Flight Check 1234 is going to execute a VFR climb."

HIA: "Flight Check 1234, Roger. How high will you be climbing?"

(Pause)

Flight Check 1234: "Until it stalls."

— Jim Murphy, jmurphy@tellink.net

"You got him on TCAS[155]? Great. When you're seven (miles) in trail[156], resume normal speed and call Chicago Center on 120.12."

Cessna: "Bay Approach, Cessna 1234 over South County Airport at four thousand feet. Request permission to land at San Jose."

Bay Approach: "Cessna 1234, Squawk 4567, and do you have Hotel?" (the current ATIS for SJC)

Cessna: "Negative, we're going to stay with my sister-in-law."

American 123: "Does your sister-in-law have any extra rooms?"

Heard while on approach to Norfolk International:

Pilot: "Norfolk Approach, N1234, VFR, 2,000 ft, landing Norfolk."

Approach: "Do you have Oscar (ATIS)?"

Pilot: "My passenger's name is Randy."

---

155 Traffic Alert & Collision Avoidance System
156 Seven miles behind

— Hicks, hicks@spacetec-inc.com

A US Air plane arriving at La Guardia from Lauderdale made a wrong turn and came nose-to-nose with a United 727. The irate ground controller (a female) lashed out at the US Air crew screaming, "US Air 2771, where are you going? I told you to turn right on Charlie taxiway; you turned right on Delta. Stop right there. I know it's difficult to tell the difference between Cs and Ds, but get it right!"

She continued, shouting hysterically, "God, you've screwed everything up; it'll take forever to sort this out. You stay right there and don't move until I tell you to. You can expect progressive taxi instructions in about a half-hour, and I want you to go exactly where I tell you, when I tell you, and how I tell you. You got that, US Air 2771?"

The airport was silent after the verbal bashing of US Air Flight 2771. No one wanted to engage the irate ground controller in her current state. Tension in every cockpit at La Guardia was running high.

Then, an unknown male pilot broke the silence and asked, "Wasn't I married to you once?"

TWAS THE NIGHT BEFORE CHRISTMAS
(Aviator's Version)

'Twas the night before Christmas, and out on the ramp,
  Not an airplane was stirring, not even a Champ.[157]
The aircraft were fastened to tie downs with care,
  In hopes that come morning, they all would be there.

The fuel trucks were nestled, all snug in their spots,

---

157 Small aircraft

With gusts from two-forty[158] at 39 knots.

I slumped at the fuel desk, now finally caught up,
And settled down comfortably, resting my butt.

When the radio lit up with noise and with chatter,
I turned up the scanner to see what was the matter.
A voice clearly heard over static and snow,
Called for clearance to land at the airport below.

He barked his transmission so lively and quick,
I'd have sworn that the call sign he used was "St. Nick."
I ran to the panel to turn up the lights,
The better to welcome this magical flight.

He called his position, no room for denial,
"St. Nicholas One, turnin' left onto final."
And what to my wondering eyes should appear,
But a Rutan[159]-built sleigh, with eight Rotax[160]Reindeer!

With vectors to final, down the glideslope he came,
As he passed all fixes, he called them by name:
"Now Ringo! Now Tolga! Now Trini and Bacun!
On Comet! On Cupid!" What pills was he takin'?

While controllers were sittin', and scratchin' their head,
They phoned to my office, and I heard it with dread,
The message they left was both urgent and dour:
"When Santa pulls in, have him please call the tower."

---

158 Compass direction
159 Burt Rutan, aircraft designer and builder
160 Aircraft engine manufacturer

He landed like silk, with the sled runners sparking,
Then I heard "Left at Charlie," and "Taxi to parking."

He slowed to a taxi, turned off of three-oh,
And stopped on the ramp with a "Ho, Ho, Ho."

He stepped out of the sleigh, but before he could talk,
I ran out to meet him with my best set of chocks.
His red helmet and goggles were covered with frost,
And his beard was all blackened from reindeer exhaust.

His breath smelled like peppermint, gone slightly stale,
And he puffed on a pipe, but he didn't inhale.
His cheeks were all rosy and jiggled like jelly,
His boots were as black as a crop-duster's belly.

He was chubby and plump, in his suit of bright red,
And he asked me to "Fill it, with a hundred low-lead."
He came dashing in from the snow-covered pump,
I knew he was anxious for drainin' the sump[161].

I spoke not a word, but went straight to my work,
And I filled up the sleigh, but I spilled like a jerk.
He came out of the restroom and sighed in relief,
Then he picked up a phone for a Flight Service brief.

And I thought as he silently scribed in his log,
These reindeer could land in an eighth-mile fog.
He completed his pre-flight, from the front to the rear,
Then he put on his headset, and I heard him yell, "Clear!"

---

161 Bladder relief

And laying a finger on his push-to-talk,
He called up the tower for clearance and squawk.
"Take taxiway Charlie, the southbound direction,
Turn right three-two-zero at pilot's discretion."

He sped down the runway, the best of the best,
"Your traffic's a Trinidad[162], inbound from the west."
Then I heard him proclaim, as he climbed through the night,
"Merry Christmas to all! I have traffic in sight."
— http://www.seawindpilots.com/
aviation_humor.htm

---

162 Small aircraft.

EIGHTEEN

Landings

Landing: a controlled collision with a planet.

Everyone already knows the definition of a "good" landing is one from which you can walk away. But few know the definition of a "great landing." It's one after which you can use the airplane another time.

It's a good landing if you can still get the doors open.

There are three simple rules for making a smooth landing. Unfortunately no one knows what they are.

"I'm not afraid of crashing. My secret is… just before we hit the ground, I jump as high as I can."
— Bill Cosby

A pilot took his grandson to the airport to watch airplanes, which always enthralled the boy. He watched, fascinated, as several airplanes took off and flew up, up, and away, into the sky. Then they spotted a plane on final. The boy asked what the plane was doing. The grandfather explained that the pilot was done flying and coming in to land now. The boy looked up with angelic eyes and said, "But if you take off, why would you ever want to land?"

We had just completed a flight in a commercial airliner from Chicago to Cedar Rapids, IA. The aircraft had taxied to the gate and the engines shut down. Everyone in the now-quiet aircraft was waiting for the seatbelt light to extinguish when my four-year-old brother's voice called out, "But, Dad! We didn't drop any bombs!"

When I was a pilot for a commuter airline, gusty winds buffeted our little plane during a landing, giving the passengers a scare. Much to everyone's relief, we touched down safely, taxied into our parking spot where ramp agents were anxiously waiting.

Unfortunately, in their haste they neglected to lock the mobile stairway firmly in place.

It was an octogenarian who got off the plane first. Walking cane in hand, he stepped on the stairway. Almost simultaneously, the wind gusted to gale force, propelling the man and stairs across the ramp toward the terminal.

We watched helplessly as they sailed over the concrete and crashed into a chain-link fence, whereupon the elderly gentleman stepped off unscathed, tipped his hat to the bystanders, and said, "Best damn service I've ever had!"

One cold January day, my mother-in-law was flying from LAX to Salt Lake City on one of those discount airlines. The weather was bad, the peanuts were stale, and the drinks were watered down. To top it off, the landing was, to put it kindly, jarring. The head flight attendant was conscious of these facts, and made it known with her last announcement to the passengers: "Thank you for your patience on this flight. You will be glad to know that we have HIT Salt Lake City."

— Cris R. Atkin

Pilot coming in with his buddy who had never flown before.

Pilot: "This is 1234 Delta five miles north for landing with Mike (ATIS)."

The tower clears him and he lands. When they shut down, the passenger, Mike, says, "Why'd you have to tell them that I was with you?"

On a flight from Montreal to Halifax, a man I know was seated next to an elderly woman whose head was bowed and whose hands were tightly clasped together. When the dinner menu was presented, she said she wouldn't have anything to eat, but would prefer to sit quietly till they landed. She added that this was her first flight, and she was terrified.

My friend, a veteran air traveler, did his best to assure her of the safety of flying. The flight was uneventful, but on touchdown the starboard wheels missed the runway, causing the plane to veer off course and head straight for the control tower.

With engines roaring, the plane lifted off again, and by just a few meters missed the control tower, whose occupants were clearly seen lying on the floor with hands over their heads.

It was a terrifying few moments, but the second approach and landing were faultless. When the engines were shut down and the passengers started to deplane, the woman unclasped her hands and smilingly looked up at my friend. "You were right," she said, "There was absolutely nothing to worry about on this flight."

The German air controllers at Frankfurt Airport are a short-tempered lot. They not only expect one to know one's parking location, but how to get there without any assistance from them. So it was with some amusement that we (a Pan Am 747) listened to the following exchange between Frankfurt ground control and a British Airways 747 (call sign Speedbird[163] 206) after landing:

Speedbird 206: "Top of the morning, Frankfurt. Speedbird 206 clear of the active runway."

Ground: "Guten morgen! You vill taxi to your gate!"

The big British Airways 747 pulled onto the main taxi way and slowed to a stop.

Ground: "Speedbird, do you not know vare you are going?"

Speedbird 206: "Stand by a moment, Ground. I'm looking up our gate location now."

Ground (with some arrogant impatience): "Speedbird 206, haff you never flown to Frankfurt before?"

Speedbird 206 (real cool): "Yes, I have; several times in 1944. In another type of Boeing. It was dark. I didn't stop."

No sooner did the flight from Philadelphia to Boston land than most passengers started unfastening their safety belts, defying the cabin crew's directions to remain seated with seatbelts fastened.

"Do I hear something?" a flight attendant asked over the PA system as the sound of clicking seatbelts filled the cabin.

"What's that sound? Okay, I'll tell the pilot to get back in the air so we can do this landing again until we get it right."

It was 1977. We were on an old DC8 Air Ceylon coming in to Colombo, Ceylon from Bangkok. The landing approach was pretty bumpy, but the biggest bump was saved for when we hit the tarmac. There was a massive shudder and shake, on at least what I hoped it was the runway.

163 Call sign for British Airways

However, we were soon airborne again and climbing steeply when a voice with a heavy Indian accent came over the PA as follows: "I'm sorry about the landing, ladies and gentlemen. The pilot will now take over."

— Tim Stuart, *Great Aviation Quotes* reader.

My wife and I were on a late evening flight from Winnipeg to Vancouver. As we began our descent, most of the passengers were either sleeping or reclining drowsily in their seats. No one was prepared for the jarring impact as the plane hit the runway.

A ripple of alarm swept through the passenger cabin, but concerned faces soon broke into smiles as the voice of the flight attendant came over the intercom: "Good evening, ladies and gentlemen. Now that we have your attention, we'd like to welcome you to Vancouver International Airport."

An airline pilot wrote that, on this particular flight, he had hammered his ship into the runway really hard. The airline had a policy that required the first officer to stand at the door while the passengers exited, give a smile, and a "Thanks for flying XYZ airline."

He said that in light of his bad landing, he had a hard time looking the passengers in the eye, thinking that someone would have a smart comment. Finally, everyone had gotten off except this little old lady walking with a cane. She said, "Sonny, mind if I ask you a question?"

"Why, no Ma'am," said the pilot. "What is it?"

The little old lady asked, "Did we land or were we shot down?"

Heard on Southwest Airlines just after a hard landing in Salt Lake City. The flight attendant came on the intercom and said, "That was quite a bump, and I know what y'all are thinking. I'm here to tell you it wasn't the airline's fault. It wasn't the pilot's fault. It wasn't the flight attendants' fault. It was the asphalt."

Overheard on a flight on a particularly windy and bumpy day: During the final approach, the Captain was really having to fight the turbulence. After an extremely hard landing, the flight attendant came on the PA and announced, "Ladies and gentlemen, welcome to Anchorage, Alaska. Please remain in your seats with your seatbelts fastened while the Captain taxis what's left of our airplane to the gate."

Another flight attendant's comment on a less than perfect landing: "We ask you to please remain seated as Captain Kangaroo bounces us to the terminal."

After a real crusher of a landing in Phoenix, the flight attendant came on with: "Ladies and Gentlemen, please remain in your seats until Captain Crash and the crew have brought the aircraft to a screeching halt against the gate. Once the tire smoke has cleared and the warning bells are silenced, we'll open the door. Then you can pick your way through the wreckage to the terminal."

After a particularly rough landing during thunderstorms in Memphis, a flight attendant on a Northwest flight announced, "Please take care when opening the overhead compartments because, after a landing like that, sure as hell everything has shifted."

On a flight back in 1997, the pilot made what can only be described as an extremely heavy landing at Luton. It was early in the morning. A number of passengers around me looked quite alarmed as, apart from the noise, a number of overhead lockers dropped open and several items of carry-on luggage were launched down the aisle.

After slowing up, the aircraft turned off the runway and turned toward the terminal. Over the PA came, "Good morning ladies gentlemen, this is Captain Smith. Welcome to Luton. And if any of you were asleep... I'll bet you're not now!"

— Contributed by Jon Wolfe

"I give that landing a 9... on the Richter scale."

LANDING RATING SCALE:

5. Marvelous, ace. Couldn't do it better myself.
4. I've seen better; just can't remember when.
3. Average. I could do better with my eyes closed.
2. You're going to log all of those (touchdowns)?
1. That wasn't a landing. That was an arrival.
0. Go get the trailer, boys.

— George Patterson

Tower: "Delta Fox Alpha, hold position. Marshall will park you."

Pilot: "Roger. Lookin' out for John Wayne."

One day the pilot of a Cherokee 180 was told by the tower to hold short of the runway while a MD80 landed. The MD80 landed, rolled out, turned around, and taxied back past the Cherokee.

Some quick-witted comedian in the MD80 crew got on the radio and said, "What a cute little plane. Did you make it all by yourself?"

Our hero, the Cherokee pilot, came back with: "I made it out of MD80 parts. Another landing like that and I'll have enough parts for another one."

Arriving ten minutes early in Indianapolis, the captain welcomed us on the PA and said, "For those who want to get their money's worth, you're welcome to stay on board for ten more minutes."

Part of a flight attendant's arrival announcement: "We'd like to thank you folks for flying with us today. And, the next time you get the insane urge to go blasting through the skies in a pressurized metal tube, we hope you'll think of US Airways."

As the plane landed and was coming to a stop at Washington National, a lone voice came over the loudspeaker: "Whoa, big fella. WHOA!"

Ground Control: "123DG, bear to the left. Disabled aircraft on the right."
Pilot: "123DG, Roger. I have the disabled aircraft in sight, but I don't see the bear yet."
— Chuck Brinson, cbrinson@tulsa.oklahoma.net

"This aircraft is equipped with a video surveillance system that monitors the cabin during taxiing. Any passengers not remaining in their seats until the aircraft comes to a full and complete stop at the gate will be strip-searched as they leave the aircraft."

As the airliner was preparing to land in Madrid in a rainstorm, an English passenger seemed noticeably afraid. "What's the problem, fellow?" asked his seat mate.
"Surely," said the Englishman, "you've heard the saying, 'The planes in Spain fall mainly in the rain!'"

A Qantas 747 landed at Paris' Charles de Gaulle airport just after the Rugby World Cup in which Australia beat France. De Gaulle has circular stands, so if an aircraft misses the turn-off, it often must taxi around again to get back to it. As the Qantas aircraft did this:

Paris ATC: "Qantas 123, are you having difficulty?"

Qantas 123: "No. Just doing a victory lap!"

The pilot of a Polish Airlines 747 is briefing his new co-pilot on landing procedures at their next destination. "This is a short runway," he says, "and I'll need all your help on the flaps, thrust reversers and brakes for this one."

The co-pilot says, "Roger that, let's go." As they approach the airfield the co-pilot says, "Boy, that's the shortest field I've ever seen." The pilot calls for half-flaps. "You have half-flaps," says the co-pilot.

As they get closer the pilot says, "Better give me 3/4 flaps."

"Roger, you have 3/4 flaps," says the co-pilot.

"Damn," says the pilot, "this looks even shorter than I remember. Give me full-flaps and standby on the brakes and thrust reversers!"

"You have full-flaps and standing by," says the co-pilot. As the wheels touch down on the runway, the pilot immediately calls for full braking and full thrust reversers.

The co-pilot complies and, as the plane comes to a shuddering stop inches from the end of the runway, the pilot, wiping sweat from his brow, says, "Holy Mother of God, that's the shortest runway I've ever seen in my life!"

"Yes," says the co-pilot looking out both windows, "but the son-of-a-bitch sure is wide!"

"Welcome to Las Vegas, Nevada. We'd like to thank you for flying Southwest Airlines. On behalf of the flight deck, we'd also like to extend a special and happy 101st birthday to a gentleman seated at the front of the aircraft." (scattered applause)

"So, if you happen to see the Captain on the way out, mind his walker, shake his hand, and wish him well for another 100 years working here at Southwest Airlines."

Please use caution when opening the overhead compartments because shift happens!

As the passengers settled in on a West Coast commuter flight, a flight attendant announced, "We'd like you folks to help us welcome our new co-pilot. He'll be performing his first commercial landing for us today, so be sure to give him a big round of applause when we come to a stop."

The plane made an extremely bumpy landing, bouncing hard two or three times before taxiing to a stop. Still, the passengers applauded. Then the attendant's voice came over the intercom, "Thanks for flying with us. And don't forget to let our co-pilot know which landing you liked best."

Flying is the second greatest thrill known to man. Landing is the first.

You can land anywhere once.

You can't go around forever. Landings are always mandatory.

You know you've landed with the wheels up when it takes full power to taxi.

After a particularly heavy landing at Jersey, (Canary Islands) the cabin attendant announced, "Will all passengers please remain in the overhead lockers until the aircraft has come to a complete halt and the seatbelt signs have been switched off."
— Glen Stansfield, Jersey European
Source: http://www.interplane.co.uk/Jokes.asp

En route to Atlanta, the plane my husband was piloting made a stop in a small town, dropped off passengers, and began taxiing back out to the runway. Just then, a flight attendant notified my husband that a man had fallen asleep and missed his stop. To save time, the crew decided to let him exit down the rear stairs, where ground transportation would be waiting to take him back to the terminal.

The other passengers watched nervously as their pilot left the cockpit to talk to a man clutching a suspiciously large briefcase. As my husband opened the rear door and let the man out, he could feel all eyes focused on him.

He slammed the door shut, brushed his hands together briskly and said, "There! Any more complaints about the food, see me!" The passengers howled.

A Southwest Flight Attendant: "Please remain in your seat with your seatbelt fastened and your seatback and tray upright until the airplane comes to a complete stop at the gate and we extinguish the seatbelt sign. There are television cameras in the cabin, so if you get up before we stop, your picture will be transmitted by satellite to Flight Attendant Central. You'll never get another bag of peanuts again."

United Airlines Flight Attendant: "Ladies and gentlemen, as you're all now painfully aware, our Captain has landed in Seattle. From all of us at United Airlines we'd like to thank you for flying with us today and please be very careful as you open the overhead bins as you may be killed by falling luggage that shifted during our so called 'touch down.'"

On landing, the flight attendant said, "Please be sure to take all of your belongings. If you're going to leave anything, please make sure it's something we'd like to have."

I was flying to Reagan National on an American Airlines flight that happened to have a run of bad luck regarding delays.

After landing about ninety minutes behind schedule, the flight attendant concluded in his, "Welcome to Reagan National Airport" announcement: "We know you have a choice in airlines, and we hope that next time your travel requires an on-time arrival, we hope you'll choose... Oh, never mind."

After the landing of a United Airlines demo ride of their new Boeing 777, the FA gave the usual announcement: "Please remain seated with your seat belts fastened until the aircraft comes to a complete stop and the captain turns off the seat belt sign. To our knowledge, no passenger has ever beaten the aircraft to the gate anyway, so you may as well stay put."

— Source: http://www.lrn2fly.com/lrn2fly/
humor_atc_al.htm.

"My brother was flying from Rochester, NY to JFK on Jet Blue. The landing was pretty hard and they bounced a bit. The flight attendant came on the PA and said, 'Damn those pot holes!'"

— Oren Katzen-268

Heard on a BA Airbus 320 flight to Hamburg after a particularly heavy landing:

"Good morning, ladies and gentlemen, this is the Captain speaking. It's normal on these occasions to blame the second pilot for any bad landing, but I cannot lie. It was me," followed by general laughter throughout the aircraft.

Captain: (after landing a bit rough)
"Ladies and gentlemen, it's happy hour. You've just received two landings for the price of one."

Overheard by a guy giving short sightseeing rides: "Sorry about the rough landing, but I'm practicing for a job at a major airline. Next time I'll try to lose your luggage."

Upon landing, the pilot warned the passengers to keep their seatbelts on because "Everyone knows I'm a great pilot, but a lousy driver."

The night flight from Washington, DC was routine until the plane landed in Indianapolis. While taxiing in from the runway, the plane suddenly came to a halt, still a considerable distance from the terminal. After sitting on the taxiway for several minutes, still waiting for the plane to move again, many passengers began to get restless.

Old pro that he was, the captain changed tension to amusement by announcing, "Ladies and gentlemen, I flew this multi-million-dollar aircraft all the way from D.C. to Indianapolis... at night... and I found the airport on my very first try!

Unfortunately, I have to wait until a guy with a couple of 99-cent flashlights shows me where to park it."

"As you exit the plane, please make sure to gather all of your belongings. Anything left behind will be distributed evenly among the flight attendants. Please don't leave children or spouses."

"Last one off the plane must clean it."